W9-BEK-416

PAINTING MURALS STEP BY STEP

Charles Grund

NORTH LIGHT BOOKS

CINCINNATI, OHIO
www.artistsnetwork.com

East Providence Public Library
~~Branch~~ Branch

751.73
Gru

B+T 6/2/03 25L

Painting Murals Step by Step. Copyright © 2003 by
Charles Grund. Manufactured in Singapore. All rights
reserved. The patterns and drawings in this book are
for the personal use of the decorative painter. By permission of the author and publisher, they may be
either hand–traced or photocopied to make single
copies, but under no circumstances may they be
resold or republished. No part of the text, patterns,
paintings or instructions, whether in whole or in part,
may be used for profit or reproduced in any form,
except as noted above, without the express written
permission of the copyright holder. No other part of
this book may be reproduced in any form or by any
electronic or mechanical means including information storage and retrieval systems without permission in writing from the publisher, except by a
reviewer, who may quote brief passages in a review.
Published by North Light Books, an imprint of F&W
Publications, Inc. 4700 East Galbraith Road, Cincinnati, Ohio 45236. (800) 289–0963. First edition.

**Library of Congress
Cataloging–in–Publication Data**

Grund, Charles.
  Painting murals step by step /
    Charles Grund.
       p. cm.
  Includes index.
  ISBN 1–58180–141–6 (pbk.) ––
  ISBN 1–58180–140–8 (hc.)
    1. Mural painting and decoration--Technique. I.
Title.

ND2550 .G78 2003
751.7'3––dc21

Edited by Maureen Mahany Berger
Designed by Joanna Detz
Interior Layout by Kathy Gardner
Production coordinated by Kristen Heller
Photography by Tim Grondin, Christine Polomsky
and Al Parrish

DEDICATION & ACKNOWLEDGMENTS

This book is dedicated to my daughter, Chloe, whose *joie de vivre*
continues to be an ever–present source
of inspiration for this old artist.

I would like to especially thank my editor, Maureen Mahany Berger,
for her tireless and enthusiastic support of my efforts.
This book could never have come about without her continued
guidance and assistance. Also, thanks to Kathy Kipp and
Greg Albert at North Light Books for their helpful involvement
in this most wonderful project.

My appreciation to Christine Polomsky, Tim Grondin, and
Al Parrish, talented photographers all, who lugged heavy equipment
all over creation in order to make so many on–site step–by–step
murals come alive on the printed page.

And my deepest appreciation to all the other talented people at
North Light Books who have helped to make this book a reality.

METRIC CONVERSION CHART

TO CONVERT	TO	MULTIPLY BY
INCHES	CENTIMETERS	2.54
CENTIMETERS	INCHES	0.4
FEET	CENTIMETERS	30.5
CENTIMETERS	FEET	0.03
YARDS	METERS	0.9
METERS	YARDS	1.1
SQ. INCHES	SQ. CENTIMETERS	6.45
SQ. CENTIMETERS	SQ. INCHES	0.16
SQ. FEET	SQ. METERS	0.09
SQ. METERS	SQ. FEET	10.8
SQ. YARDS	SQ. METERS	0.8
SQ. METERS	SQ. YARDS	1.2
POUNDS	KILOGRAMS	0.45
KILOGRAMS	POUNDS	2.2
OUNCES	GRAMS	28.4
GRAMS	OUNCES	0.04

3 1499 00357 5872

Photo by Neil Reck

Charles Grund has been working as a professional artist and educator for over twenty years. He received his BFA in painting from Washington University in St. Louis and his MFA in painting from the University of Cincinnati. In addition to his work as a muralist, he has taught many Fine Art and Art History courses over the years. His murals can be found in private residences, restaurants, public libraries, corporate offices, conference centers, and many other facilities. He has been featured on the syndicated TV program, *Around the House*, with Jay Shatz.

Charles exhibits his own paintings, and his work is included in collections in the United States and abroad.

Charles lives with his wife, Julie, and his daughter, Chloe, in Cincinnati.

WORDS TO LIVE BY

The late Walter Farmer, an extraordinary interior designer and gentleman here in Cincinnati, gave me the following three points of advice about starting your own business:

*Always be on time.
Always be honest.
Always do your very best work.*

I can't think of any better or wiser advice to give someone.

TABLE OF CONTENTS

This book is intended for anyone interested in mural painting, from the novice to the well–initiated, from the casual viewer to the active participant. My intention has been to present my working methods as plainly and as clearly as possible, with the hope that readers may find useful information to apply to their own experiences. As you will see, I work in a rather straightforward manner, and often I try to suggest things more than actually render them in great detail. Rather than simple laziness, more often than not this relates to the time constraints that are part of most commissions. The artist who has no limits on time or budget is a lucky but rare bird, indeed!

By following some of the procedures in this book, you will learn some easy ways to render different things in a convincing manner. It's always important for beginners to keep in mind that a large part of creating three–dimensional illusion on a two–dimensional surface depends on draftsmanship. If you don't understand the fundamentals of drawing, then you will have a tougher time making forms and spatial relationships believable. Don't despair. A little practice can go a long way. When you draw objects, make sure that you know where your line is in space and, when lines intersect, be clear about which line is closest to the viewer. Pay special attention to the five components of light upon an object (see page 29). This can be applied to many different situations. I emphasize this to underscore the fact that many beginners may find painting easier than drawing or vice versa. With experience comes improvement and balance between both disciplines.

I have always tried to do the best work possible and to find enjoyment therein. Let's face it—a lot of mural work is pure physical labor...transporting materials, setting things up, getting prepared and mixing paints. Much of it is busy work or running around or making phone calls. But as soon as you begin sketching on a wall, everything else should fade into the background. You are creating an entire universe out of nothing; you are the writer, director, actor and audience rolled into one. What a great thing that is! And if you can get paid for doing such enjoyable work...how wonderful! My wish is that this book will provide enough information to inspire you to do beautiful mural painting on your own. Finding out where your strengths lie is an important part of growing as an artist—learning what to emphasize and what to avoid. Allowing yourself room for mistakes is very wise and even comforting. Just be sure to step back often and take an honest look at your work.

It is with great pleasure that I present this book to you. May you find much within to enjoy and also many years of glorious mural painting ahead...and many solid commissions to boot!

STARTING OUT

Don't quit your day job just yet! Becoming a muralist takes more than artistic ability. It also takes some business skills for which many artists are not well equipped. As always, it helps to speak with someone experienced in the field. However, not all muralists will be willing to lend advice. Don't be discouraged if this happens to you. There are many muralists out there and the competition can be intense. It will take some time to get established and to find a way to set yourself apart—to find a niche for yourself. Some specialize in children's murals; others specialize in *trompe l'oeil* or graphics. Make sure that you understand what it is that you do best and try to move in that direction.

Before getting business cards printed, you will need a portfolio—something to show to potential clients. For the most part, mural jobs come about in two ways—through interior designers and by word of mouth. Most designers already have an artist or artists who can be contacted for mural work. (Some designers never include murals in their work.) They will let you know right away if they are open to working with you by whether or not they ask to see examples of your work. Word of mouth, obviously, comes later, after some of your work is up and being seen.

You must have photographs of your mural work. If you have none, then figure out some way to produce at least a few murals that you can photograph and then round out with some drawings, designs or smaller paintings on paper. Paint a mural on your own wall for starters, then try painting for family and friends. Paint smaller designs on boards and photograph them. Whatever you can do to showcase your talents, make a strong effort to gather a portfolio of images for presentation. Try to keep the photographs a consistent size and quality, preferably arranged in a presentation portfolio. You can find portfolios in art stores but they can be quite costly. If you're not ready to spend that kind of money yet, then get a photo album that is neutral in design. Don't overdo your presentation: If you can't afford an expensive portfolio, then keep it plain and simple. Concentrate on the quality of your art and the photographs you take.

Once you have this ready, compile a list of designers and either telephone them and request a meeting, or send them a cover letter letting them know when you will be calling to request a meeting. Be sure to follow through with the call. The chances are great that you will get their voice mail. A good friend of mine, who is now a successful entrepreneur, told me that, when she was starting out, she never left voice mail messages because she didn't want that person to know she had called repeatedly. She kept calling until the other person answered in person. You'll have to decide what you want to do. It takes time. When you do reach someone, be friendly but brief and to the point. Do not offer too much information. Simply ask them if you can meet with them to show examples of your work. Let them ask about your experience—it might not even come up.

Getting work requires patience and persistence. Even after you have established yourself, there will be some weeks that are busier than others. This is part of being self–employed. You may want to try a few jobs on the side first to "test the waters" before plunging in full time.

PAPERWORK

Once you are into it full time, you will need the appropriate materials and a filing method to keep track of things. Computers are great for this and you can buy business software that includes contracts, invoices, letterheads and even business cards. If you do not have a computer, then you can find most of what you need at an office supply store. There you will find packs of carbonless proposal forms, on which to write out your contracts, and carbonless invoice forms to mail out for balances due. Once a client or designer has agreed to your services, you need to get a written contract in hand, signed and dated by the person paying the bill. Write out a description of the job as clearly and completely as possible on the contract, including anything that you are or are not responsible for. For example, if any furniture needs to be moved, identify who is responsible for moving it; if changes are made later, outline the additional charges as appropriate; if there are defects in the wall, identify who is to fix them; and so on. Also, make clear the terms of payment. It is wise and acceptable to ask for a deposit in advance. Some muralists ask for a third as an advance, some for half. Then decide if the final payment is due upon completion, or a week later, or whenever. Some design firms operate on a thirty–day pay schedule. It helps to inquire in advance.

Proposal forms have three copies per form. Keep the bottom one and send the top two to the client, requesting that the client send back a signed and dated copy with the deposit.

If the mural job requires a lot of preparatory work, such as a finished drawing or small–scale painting, decide in advance if that is to be charged separately or as part of the basic cost of doing the mural. Perhaps you will do a preliminary sketch but then tell the client that additional sketches require extra charges at so much per hour.

Also, buy an address book that has large calendar pages and note pages, as well as places to put names, addresses, and phone numbers. This is the "daily planner" that becomes essential for keeping track of clients, references, interior designers, businesses, and on–site notes for preparing bids. Keeping all of this information in one place for easy access is invaluable.

A business card is helpful to have. It gives you something that you can leave after a meeting. Brochures are great to have but are costly. If you produce one yourself on your computer, make sure that it looks completely professional. Let an impartial observer check it out and give you an opinion. The idea is to look successful and professional.

WRITING BIDS

It is important to have a written or oral bid before accepting a mural job. This is the declaration of how much the job will cost, presented as a single cost, or broken down into parts, such as labor and materials. Its presentation depends on you or on the job requirements. Many clients are satisfied with the final cost and don't need a breakdown into bid components.

Bidding is an inexact art form that requires some experience to do well. First, decide how much you wish to make per hour, keeping in mind your overhead and self–employment taxes. Next, measure the area to be painted and get a rough idea of the square footage. (Don't forget to subtract for doors, windows, etc.) Let's say our mural is 8 feet x 8 feet or 64 square feet. Estimate how much time you think the job will take. Break the job down into steps and estimate time for each: setting up and prep work, layout, roughing–in the design, initial painting; final painting and detailing, and removing equipment. Experience makes this easier and less like guesswork.

Never do a mural job without a contract, unless the job is for a close friend or a family member.

All of this should be done on a clean sheet of paper, in your daily planner or on your computer, clearly labeled with the job name and date. Keep this for later reference.

Often, I do three bids: low, medium and high. Then, I choose the one that I think will get the job. I figure bids based on my hourly rate, day rate, and square footage rates and compare them. Sometimes they are close; other times they differ widely.

If, for example, you decide on $50 as your hourly rate (which translates into a day rate of $400), and you figure that the job will take you about thirty hours to do, then do the following:

$50 X 30 hours = $1500 for LABOR only.

Next, use your day rate in the equation:

$400 X 4 days (day equivalent of 30 working hours) = $1600

Then add the material costs to both figures. Keep this figure very general—don't get caught up in the exact dollars and cents of everything:

$1500 + 175 = $1675 (@ hourly rate)

$1600 + 175 = $1775 (@ day rate)

In addition to these figures, figure out your square footage price. This is tricky and usually depends on your ability to match levels of difficulty to the square foot price. Most muralists I know charge from $10 to $50 per square foot—quite a range. Let's pick the middle—$30/square foot:

$30 X 64 square feet = $1920

This is higher than the other two figures. If you go with the hourly or day rate, you will be charging a price that seems reasonable both for compensating yourself and for enabling you to get the job. Using these three figures, you can bid lower when you need the work and higher when you're busy and don't need it as much. This is an inexact science, and most mural artists have a horror story or two about underbidding a job. Experience will make it easier.

Abstract A work of art arrayed pictorially without a recognizable subject matter, the emphasis being on formal aspects.

Achromatic A colorless scheme using blacks, whites and grays.

Acrylic Water–based, permanent paint composed of pigments suspended in a synthetic resin.

Acrylic gesso Water–based primer formulated for use with acrylic paints. Also works under oil paints. Not to be confused with traditional gesso.

Aerial perspective Tendency of forms to become increasingly paler, bluer and more blurred as they recede in space.

Aggressive Warm colors: reds, oranges and yellows.

Alkyds Quick–drying oil paints made by a complicated process combining oil and synthetic resins.

Aquaglaze A water-based glazing medium.

Binder The substance in paints that holds the pigment particles together and attaches them to the support.

Blending Softening the juncture between two colors until they appear to merge.

Bristle brush A brush made from the stiff hairs of an animal, usually a hog.

Cartoon A detailed and often full–scale drawing done for a painting; transferred by rubbing, scaling or pouncing the image.

Cast shadow The area of shadow thrown onto the surrounding space by the illumination of an object.

Charcoal The carbonaceous material made by charring twigs of willow or vine in a vacuum.

Cheesecloth Loosely woven cotton fabric originally used in cheese making.

Chroma The degree of saturation or intensity of a color.

Complementary colors Pairs of colors that are exactly opposed on the color wheel and create gray when mixed.

Cotton duck An artist's canvas material made from cotton that is less expensive than linen.

Denatured alcohol Alcohol that has been rendered undrinkable and is used as a solvent.

Diluent A liquid or solvent used to thin (dilute) a prepared color; water for acrylics and latex paints; mineral spirits or turpentine for oils.

Dry–brush technique A painting method in which fairly stiff paint is stroked across the painting surface leaving openings in the paint film; highly influenced by the surface texture.

Earth colors Various pigments consisting mostly of iron oxides and leaning toward a brownish hue; made from refined clays and minerals dug from the ground.

Emulsion A permanent mixture of ordinarily nonmixable substances, like oil and water.

Extender An inert chemical substance added to paint primarily to increase volume and also to lower cost.

Ferrule The metal sleeve holding the hairs of a brush in place.

Filbert A type of artist's brush with flattened bristles that curve slightly on both sides at the top.

Flat An artist's brush with a flattened, squared–off end.

Fresco True fresco is a technique of wall painting where the colors are painted directly into a wet layer of lime plaster, forming a bond.

Frottage The technique of rubbing with a pigmented substance.

Fugitive A term applied to pigments that are impermanent and have poor light-fastness.

Gesso A painting ground for rigid supports, made from chalk and glue sizing; not to be confused with acrylic gesso.

Glaze A mixture of medium and transparent color laid over a dried underpainting.

Glaze medium A vehicle into which transparent color is mixed to make a glaze; the vehicle imparts luminosity, better brushing ability and ease of paint manipulation.

Grisaille A monochromatic painting done in various tones of gray.

Ground The surface onto which paint is applied.

Highlight The brightest part of the painted subject.

Hue The specifically designated name of a color.

Impasto Painting with thickly applied paint; creating textured effects.

Imprimatura A translucent "veil" or wash of thinned color over the ground; used as a base for further painting.

Inorganic Nonorganic; a chemical not derived from living matter.

Intensity The strength of a color.

Key color The dominant color in a color scheme or mixture.

Light The illuminated part of a subject.

Lightfastness How a pigment performs when exposed to light.

Linear perspective A system for representing volume and depth on a flat surface using lines that converge at a vanishing point on a horizon line.

Local color The actual color of a subject when seen under ideal light conditions.

Masking Use of tape, paper, plastic, or other material to protect and/or isolate a particular area of a painting or surroundings on which paint is not wanted.

Matte Having a dull or nonreflective surface.

Medium The actual material or type of paint being used or a substance added to the paint to change its consistency and/or characteristics.

Monochromatic Painting with various tones of a single color.

Motif A recurring subject, theme or idea in a work or series of works.

Nylon brushes Brushes with bristles that are made of nylon—a thermoplastic polyamide.

Oil paint Paint made by grinding pigments with an oil medium, such as linseed or safflower oil.

Opaque Not transparent or translucent. In opaque painting, highlights are made by the addition of white paint.

Optical mixing Two or more juxtaposed colors that merge optically into a single color; a technique used by the Impressionists and Pointillists.

Organic Composed of or related to living compounds.

Panel A rigid painting support made from a stable or non-warping material, such as Masonite, MDF board, certain hardwoods, and laminated materials.

Perspective A technique for depicting three-dimensional space on a flat surface.

Picture plane The imagined upright plane separating the viewer from the subject. This translates into the picture's actual surface.

Pigment A coloring substance.

Plane The area of a two-dimensional surface, having defined limits of size and spatial position.

Porosity The degree of absorbency.

Primary colors Red, yellow and blue.

Primer A substance applied to a support to render it less absorbent and also isolate it from the paint film.

Receding Cool colors: greens, blues and violets.

Reflected light The light that bounces back into the shadowed part of a subject.

Round An artist's brush with bristles that are formed into a round shape.

Saturation The intensity of a color.

Scumbling A painting technique in which opaque but thin colors are dragged over an underpainted area of contrasting color, allowing some of the underpainting to show through.

Secondary colors Two primary colors mixed together: green, orange and violet.

Shadow The lack of illumination on a subject; the transition to shadow in painting often involves the addition of gray or the complementary color.

Solvent Ordinarily a liquid substance used to thin another substance or dissolve it into a solution.

Stipple A technique of tapping the tips of a brush's bristles against the paint surface for textural effect.

Stretcher A wooden frame over which a canvas or similar support is stretched using tacks or staples.

Support The surface used for painting.

Tertiary (intermediate) colors; one primary and one secondary color mixed together.

Tint Color mixed with white.

Tone The degree of lightness or darkness of a color.

Toned ground An opaque, colored ground to paint on.

Transparent painting A painting method using transparent colors whose effects depend on the whiteness of the ground or the tonalities of the underpainting.

Trompe l'oeil Painted illusions intended to fool the eye into believing that the two-dimensional imagery actually exists in three dimensions.

Underdrawing Drawing done before painting, usually with charcoal or greatly thinned paint.

Underpainting Preliminary painting that can include washes or blocked-in areas over which further painting can proceed.

Varnish Special preparations applied to painted surfaces to impart a protective surface film.

Vehicle The binding medium in which pigment is ground.

Wet-on-wet The application of paint onto an already wet paint.

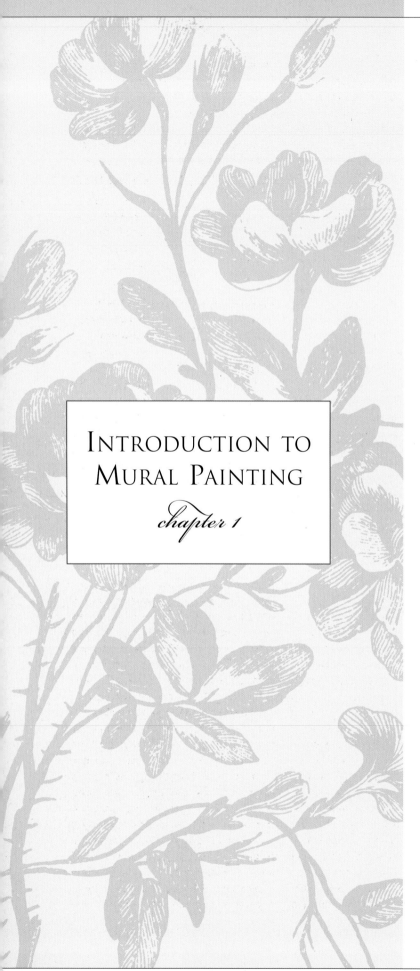

INTRODUCTION TO MURAL PAINTING
chapter 1

KINDS OF MURAL PAINTING

Many kinds of murals exist in vastly different settings around the world. Some are astonishingly complex and some are small, simple and intimate. The context of the mural's location usually influences the subject matter, scale, color and design. You may have been in a government building at some time—perhaps a post office—that has one of the many WPA-sponsored murals created between the world wars. The subject was probably historical or educational and painted in a style clearly intelligible to the viewer, reflecting the governmental context. Imagine this type of mural in your living room. It might seem too formal and stiff, lacking the relaxed intimacy that you may want in your home. Yet in the environment of a government building, the WPA mural functions suitably. Conversely, a mural of a delicate flowering vine growing on a softly painted trellis might seem too precious for the formal setting of the post office.

Murals may be found in homes, restaurants, clubs, office buildings, stores, museums, zoos, houses of worship, an endless variety of locations. Some murals are painted in a representational style meant to fool the eye—the meaning of the commonly-used French term *trompe l'oeil*. For example, a wall which appears to open up onto a veranda. Other murals are purely decorative and nonrepresentational—sometimes consisting of patterns and colors composed on a wall (often seen in restaurants). Some murals appeal to children, employing brighter colors and large, simple, easy-to-understand forms (see the Map Room on page 133). In corporate settings, murals often reflect the image that the company wishes to convey to its clientele, or some related historical elements of significant value (see the CSX mural on page 132).

WHERE TO PLACE A MURAL

Choosing the site of a mural is obviously a different task for the professional muralist working for a client than for an artist planning a mural for himself. For a professional, the mural's location has, in most cases, already been selected, and it is the artist's job to design something appropriate to that site. This is not always the case, of course; sometimes the muralist is asked to make suggestions. When you are choosing a site for a mural, keep in mind the following.

Need

What part of the house could benefit the most from adding a mural, in terms of becoming a focal point? Keep in mind that painted murals are attention getters. Some of this entails deciding who the intended audience is: yourself and your family, partner, roommate or visitors. Certainly, all can enjoy your mural, but if, for example, you have entertaining in mind, you don't want to choose a bedroom. Guest bathrooms are great places to start because they are much smaller and less formal than, say, living rooms.

Size

How ambitious are you feeling? Planning and designing a mural is one thing; executing it is another altogether. Your level of experience should be the deciding factor in this regard. It may be better to start small and work your way up to a more challenging scale later on. However, if you have decided to start in a bathroom that is tiny and cramped, you may want to consider a site that allows more physical comfort as well as room to step back a bit for evaluation. Keep in mind two things: the mural has to work as a totality—a unified image—so the artist must be able to comprehend the whole; and the amount of paint needed may be surprising and/or expensive (unless commercial latex is used).

Accessibility

Some places are harder to reach than others, but even seemingly accessible sites may prove difficult once the work begins. It always pays to give each site a thorough visual examination in advance. Ask yourself some pertinent questions:

1. Can all areas that need masking or covering be reached?

2. Is there room for a ladder if one is needed?

3. Is there some place to keep materials while working?

4. Will you be blocking the access of others?

5. How far away is access to water and/or a utility sink?

Available Light

Ordinarily, I prefer to paint murals using the available light, meaning the lighting conditions that are pre-existing on site—whether natural or artificial light or a combination of both. Natural light is almost always the best, but it fluctuates with weather conditions and the time of day, so some artificial light is often needed at some point. Even rooms with a great many windows will vary according to the directional source of the sunlight. (Artists usually prefer northern light because it is the most even, least fluctuating light.) If the available light is not sufficient for you, add some light of your own but be sensitive to how it changes the appearance of things. For example, strong halogen work lights tend to bleach out colors, making it harder to see correctly the colors you're mixing. Thus you might overcompensate and make your mixtures too bright, too warm, too cool and so on. If you use a halogen work light (as I do), get one that has an adjustable stand and try aiming it at the ceiling near the wall you're working on, so that the light can spread out and reflect on your wall rather than hit it directly.

SOURCE MATERIALS

If you are undecided as to the subject of your mural, there are countless sources of inspiration. We are fortunate to live in a time when all kinds of images are relatively easy to access through books, videos, magazines and the Internet as well as museums. The entire history of art is at our fingertips and it can be quite helpful to look at accomplished paintings to see how artists throughout history have expressed themselves and solved the problems inherent in working on a large, flat surface. Photographic sources can be inspiring as well. You might see something in a magazine that sparks an idea. It's wise to tear out the page and set it aside for later reference.

Always keep in mind, however, that copyrighted images are not yours to copy; they are the property of the person who made them. There are inexpensive paperback books available that are filled with copyright-free images from the past. And there are technical or scientific books from which you can find images to help, say, render a particular animal.

I have many clients who show me many images to help describe what they have in mind for a mural. One might be a particular landscape, either painted or photographed; another might be a photograph showing something entirely different that they want included somehow. With practice you can become quite adept at combining many different ideas into a single, unified image.

If you're unfamiliar or a little rusty with art history, set aside some time for yourself at a good library—a university or museum library—to relax and browse through some mural and painting books.

STYLE

Having a style and being conscious of your own style are two different things. Each of us makes a unique imprint on whatever means of expression we undertake: a particular way of making lines, for example, or a tendency to use crisp, highly organized patterns as opposed to more spontaneous and scattered forms. Recognizing the strong and weak points of your own artmaking is something that takes time, experience and a willingness to critique yourself often. If you do not have lots of experience, then you can begin by recognizing the specific ways in which your favorite images are composed and relating these observations to commonly understood elements of style:

1. Classical or traditional—Forms are rendered in a strongly three-dimensional way, within deep space clearly delineated by perspective; the composition is tightly organized in a logical manner; the

Classical

Impressionistic

Expressionistic

Nonrepresentational

Imitative

NOTE:
All examples shown here
are monochromatic.

light source is easy to see and it not only helps solidify the forms but also sets the mood; a story or specific meaning may be conveyed; color is subdued with occasional accents.

2. Impressionistic—Forms are broken up into small brushstrokes and may be defined only by changes in color and value, not line; color is broken and mixed by the eye, not on the surface; color is lighter and brighter; the light source is not necessarily easy to spot.

3. Expressionistic or fantastical—Forms and colors are exaggerated; the subject matter may be other-worldly or difficult to decipher; the light source may be unclear or may seem to emanate from within.

4. Nonrepresentational—Forms and colors represent themselves, not recognizable objects; composition is achieved without necessarily relating to the familiar visual world.

5. Imitative—Painting with the purpose of reproducing the "look" of another era or style.

6. Monochromatic—The use of a single color or color scheme, for example, a cityscape painted entirely in warm grays.

PURPOSE

As stated previously, a mural easily becomes the focal point of a room. This can be positive or negative, depending on what purpose the mural is intended to serve. In a dining room, for example, most people want to be surrounded with a certain formality that still provides comfort and nurtures and enhances the social interaction of dining without intruding. A mural is a wonderful way to do this, yet if the mural is too strong—either visually or by subject—then the dining experience could be impaired. Imagine trying to eat while surrounded by circus animals or battle scenes or colors so bright and jarring that indigestion becomes the theme. I couldn't begin to count the number of times I've been unable to enjoy a meal at a restaurant because of loud music. Visual imagery

can have a strong influence as well.

Generally, a mural should enhance the existing surroundings, not compete with them. Subject matter, style and color scheme should relate to the purpose and the decorative treatment of the space(s) under consideration. Professional muralists often work with interior designers and, in most instances, the designer will present the artist with paint and fabric samples to ensure that everything works well together. When working without a designer, it's important to be sensitive to these design issues and to take the time to consider how the mural will relate to the environment.

In the majority of cases, a client wants a mural that will beautify a space or series of spaces without dominating the overall design. The purpose is to beautify, which is always a subjective enterprise. Thus the elements of style become the focal point and you must be sensitive to and specific about your choices of color, subject, composition and so on.

If the purpose is to relate a particular theme or to glorify certain historical elements, then you need to be prepared to do research. If you are working with a client, be certain to ask lots of questions in advance about what is expected.

Subject

Choosing a subject for a mural can be made easier if you do some advance preparation. First, you should answer the following questions:

1. What is the primary use of the room?

2. Who will see the mural? Knowing the audience, what sort of things do they like? Conversely, what do they not like?

3. What is the architecture of the space? Can it be worked into the mural?

4. Does the intended audience want a mural firmly anchored in familiar territory or one that transports them into another world?

5. Should the mural work within the spatial limitations of the site or create the illusion of expanded space?

6. Does a specific idea need to be expressed?

7. What constraints exist because of the interior design of the space? For example, a room designed with an emphasis on period furniture may limit the choices of subject in a way that a more eclectically furnished room might not.

Once you have answered these preliminary questions, begin brainstorming ideas—tossing around and writing down as many ideas as possible. Then narrow the list to fit more closely to the limitations imposed by the answers to your questions.

At the same time, spread your resource materials out over a tabletop and look at them for inspiration. If you have original sketches or designs, you should look at them as well. Either way, the goal is to have as many good options as possible to choose from. In this manner, you can select a proper subject without having a nagging feeling that something better or more suitable may have been overlooked.

The choice of subject will influence the design of the mural in many ways. If the mural includes architectural elements, then composing the picture will involve an almost mathematical approach with the use of perspective, lots of measuring and mechanical drawing tools and so forth. If it is purely a landscape painting, then fewer mechanical means are needed.

PREPARATION
& MATERIALS
chapter 2

KINDS OF SURFACES

Fixed

Murals are generally painted on a fixed, immovable surface. These vary greatly in terms of relative smoothness and integrity. I have painted murals on rough stucco surfaces as well as newly skim-coated walls that are as smooth as can be.

When faced with the surface on which you plan to paint, the first thing to do is to make a thorough visual inspection of it. If it is a painted wall, which is the most common, look for large cracks, the kinds of stains that might leak through your paint film such as stains from water or mold, and flaking or peeling paint that might prevent the mural from sticking. Large cracks must be filled with a good quality spackling material, sanded, primed and basecoated with the wall paint, all before the mural work begins. Stains should be coated with good stain-proofing primer and then covered with wall paint. Flaking or peeling paint needs to be scraped and/or sanded, spackled or skim coated with wall mud, primed and base painted. Smaller hairline cracks and other imperfections do not always need to be attended to as the mural paint will cover some of this and the mural imagery will usually disguise it as well.

Always consult with a reputable paint store with a knowledgeable staff. If the sales clerk responds to your questions by reading the label on a paint can, then seek out someone else. They obviously don't know their stuff.

The wall must also be inspected for dirt or dust and, if it is newly constructed, tested for drywall dust. In many newly constructed homes, drywall dust can filter from room to room. A dusty wall should be wiped down with a clean rag. An extremely dirty or greasy wall should be cleaned with a warm, soapy water solution, then wiped down with a clean wet rag and allowed to dry.

Previously painted walls must be checked to determine if oil or water-based paints have been used. To find out: take a clean rag slightly dampened with denatured alcohol and rub the surface in an inconspicuous spot. Many paint stores sell small packets containing a pre-soaked cloth. If the paint begins to come off, then latex water-based paint has been used. If you are using oil paints for the mural, then you can paint on either surface. However, water-based paints must be used over a water-based ground. If your wall is coated with an oil-based paint and you plan to paint with acrylics or latex paints, then you need to seal that oil layer with a primer and apply a new latex basecoat. Fortunately, water-based paints have come a long way in the past decade. There are new products on the market that make many jobs much easier. Benjamin Moore's *Fresh Start*, for instance, is an excellent latex primer intended to stick to almost any surface, allowing for a recoating with latex paints.

It is also important to differentiate among the sheens of commercial paints. Commonly, they are, from lowest to highest sheen: flat, eggshell, satin, semigloss and gloss. (Benjamin Moore has a pearl finish between eggshell and satin.)

Some paint companies have their own trade nicknames for different sheens and some have a limited variety, such as "low sheen" or "high sheen." The sheen represents how shiny and absorbent the paint finish is. This is a very important factor in choosing paint. Trying to paint a mural on a surface that is too absorbent or too slick can be an exercise in frustration. Flat paint should be avoided at all times unless it is one of the newer water-based paints that have been strengthened by additives such as Teflon (Porter) or ceramic molecules (Miller Brothers' *Aqua Borne Ceramic*). Since flat paint absorbs greatly, your brush full of paint will be stopped short in its tracks, as opposed to a slicker surface where the brush will glide along controllably. A highly glossy surface is also troublesome as paint will tend to run and not adhere well enough. If this is what you have to work with, then sand the surface with a fine-grit sandpaper before you start. A satin, pearl or semigloss finish is suitable for most mural work.

Occasionally, the wall in question is covered with wallpaper. Like any surface, it should be examined carefully: How well is it sticking? What do the seams look like? Are they abutted or overlapping or are they coming loose? Is the surface too slick? You can paint over wallpaper provided that it is in good condition, but I would recommend applying a bonding primer (e.g., Fresh Start) and

basecoat first.

If the surface is wood or metal (murals often include smaller areas like this), or some kind of synthetic material like plastic, inspect it to see if it has been painted and if it is in good condition. If it's painted, then you must determine whether oil- or water-based paint was used. If the painted surface is in good condition and compatible with your paint, then you can proceed with perhaps just a little sanding. A high-gloss sheen must be sanded first. Commonly found items of this type are light switch and outlet covers (almost always plastic) and ductwork covers (usually metal but sometimes wood). I have found that the best way to prepare these for inclusion in the mural is to remove them and lay them on a sheet of cardboard resting on plastic sheeting or a drop cloth. Pushing the screws separately into the board, so that only the head sticks up. Then I spray everything with a quick-dry bonding primer from an aerosol can like B.I.N. (see page 30). After this dries, usually in half an hour or so, a basecoat (preferably the same paint that the wall is coated with) can be brushed on. I use a small, flat nylon brush, 3/4-inch (19mm) to 1-inch (25mm). When this dries, the cover can be screwed back into place.

Movable

Sometimes a mural job may require the use of a moveable support, meaning one that is freestanding and transportable. Ordinarily, canvas that is either stretched over a frame or tacked temporarily onto a wall or panel is used. The advantage of a moveable support is that it can be worked on anywhere and then, once it is installed, it can usually be uninstalled later if desired. Canvas can be attached to a wall somewhat like wallpaper; it is advisable, however, to hire a professional wallpaper hanger for this task, unless you have experience. The stretched canvas needs to be fit into a recess of some sort, as it has noticeable depth. Panels also need special treatment for installation, depending on their thickness. They can be glued into place as well as nailed or screwed, which obviously necessitates

some touch-up.

As stated, moveable supports give you the advantage of mobility. But working away from the mural's eventual location removes the advantage of being engaged, not only with the mural itself, but also with its context—the surroundings to which it needs to relate. In the event that you have an out-of-town commission for which you are unable to travel, then a moveable support becomes a necessity. I always prefer to work on preprimed canvas, tacked to my studio wall. When finished, I roll the canvas around a sturdy cardboard tube, wrap it well or put it into another, larger tube, and then ship it.

In most situations, I like to let the client know about the option of a moveable (i.e., removable) support. It is an added expense, both for the additional materials and for the installation.

MATERIALS

There is no overstating the importance of having the right materials for a mural job. And, it is just as important to have the right quality of materials. There are certain things that can be had for a relatively low cost. But, in general, it pays to use the better stuff.

Prep Materials
It's important to know how to prepare a room or rooms for painting. The more familiar you become with this part of the job, the easier and quicker it will become. The following are basic prep materials.

Plastic sheeting 2-mil thickness is good for most jobs. If you plan to do a lot of mural work, then it's best to buy a large roll, which comes in a long box (as opposed to small, folded plastic drop cloths in packages). It is available at paint stores and large home supply stores such as Home Depot.

Statically-charged masking film This comes in different-sized, pre-folded rolls (3M brand is best) and is made for use with a hand masking machine. It can be

Miscellaneous large painting supplies include various-sized ladders, levels, scaffolding, buckets, small metal trays used as palettes, an extension cord, scissors, a foam knee pad, rags, plastic sheeting, a hair dryer, a respirator, buckets, lights, latex gloves and storage boxes.

used with or without the masker and is good for protecting walls, drapery, mantles, and furniture from splatter, etc. It clings to surfaces, so it only needs to be taped at the top.

Tape Tape comes in many sizes. Regardless of size, always use "safe-release" tape. It employs glue that will not adhere too much, so that you won't accidentally ruin a surface. The blue tape has more sticking power and is good for surfaces that are less vulnerable: metal, plastic, varnish and oil- or gloss-painted surfaces, for example. It is also good for using on carved or intricate surfaces that need masking. The white tape has less sticking power and should be used where the surface is more likely to pull

off: flat painted walls and wallpaper are good examples. (Again, the 3M brand is good.) Avoid regular masking tape.

Drop cloths It helps to have large drop cloths—9' x 12' (2.75m x 3.65m) and/or 12' x 15' (3.65m x 4.5m)—as well as smaller runners that are good for hallways—4' x 15' (1.2m x 4.m). Drop cloths come in different materials—canvas and synthetic—and prices. The biggest decision to make is whether or not to get them with an extra protective coating. I believe you can't have too much protection and I usually go for this type. However, even these can allow fluids to pass through; for this reason, I put plastic sheeting down first.

General Materials

Ladders There are many types of ladders available and they are classified according to their usage (household vs. commercial) and their structural strength. Household ladders are not strong enough for professional use. Class II ladders hold up to 225 pounds, which is fine for most people. Class I ladders are extra heavy duty and can hold about fifty pounds more. Ladders are available in wood, aluminum and fiberglass. Wood ladders tend to get wobbly after a while. Aluminum ones are nice because of their light weight, but keep in mind that they can conduct electricity. Fiberglass ladders do not conduct electricity but are more expensive and slightly heavier. I

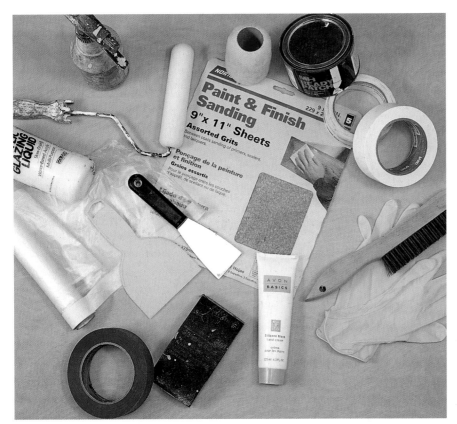

Miscellaneous smaller supplies include painter's tape, Avon's *Silicone Glove* hand cream, sandpaper, spackle, a sanding block, masking tape, a spray bottle filled with water, a paint roller and covers in various sizes, latex gloves, spackling knives, plastic sheeting and glazing liquid.

use a tiny two-foot (.6m) wooden ladder (cheap to buy and handy to have), a five-foot (1.52m) Class I ladder (fits nicely in the car) and a Little Wing ladder—an aluminum multiuse ladder that can be a step ladder, extension ladder or an uneven surface ladder. It also splits into two small A-frame ladders. The Little Wing takes the place of other ladders but is extremely heavy and cumbersome to move around.

Scaffolding At one time or other, most professional muralists are faced with a job that requires reaching extreme heights. On some of these jobs, you can use two extension ladders and a walkboard—either 14 inches (35.5cm) or 20 inches (50.8cm) wide—which stretches between them on top of ladder jacks.

This setup has to be used with great care as it can be very unstable. The feet of the two ladders, in particular, must be stabilized. On stairs, I often use a tall step ladder on the landing and a shorter step ladder at the top of the stairs and place a thin walkboard on the rungs, stretching between the two ladders (never on the top of the ladders). This, however, does not always reach high enough. When ladders won't work, scaffolding will usually do the job. I own a small five-foot high (1.5m) collapsible scaffold that is easy to transport and very handy. It has two adjustable shelves on which to stand or set materials and the wheels have foot brakes. This kind of scaffolding is relatively affordable. For larger jobs, I rent my scaffolding and add this cost into the bid. This kind of scaffolding can

be delivered for a reasonable price and comes in sections of various sizes: heights (each section) from 3 feet (.9m) to 6 feet (1.8m) and widths of 29 inches (73.7cm) and 60 inches (152.4 cm). The 29-inch (73.7cm) wide version works well for most jobs and is easier to build and move about. For very high jobs, where strength really matters, the wider scaffolding is the better choice. The sections can be stacked and there are guardrails available for protection. Also, wheel extenders are available. They fit between the wheel and the scaffolding and can be turned to gradually raise the scaffolding, which is helpful if you need only an extra foot or so.

Containers It's helpful to have resealable plastic containers on hand to mix paints, hold water or solvents, temporarily store paint and so on. I use the kind that have printed measurements on the side (1 pint, 2 1/2 quarts, 5 quarts) because they're sturdy, easy to use and clean, and the tops seal fairly well. For longer storage, buy empty commercial metal paint cans and lids. Plastic kitchen storage containers—the kind that come packaged four or five together—are also great to use for mixing and storing paint and are reasonably priced as well.

Rags Most artists need lots of rags. They should be sturdy, soft, cotton and, most of all, lint-free. I buy 100 pounds at a time from a professional rag vendor. The large home building chain stores have rags in boxes, usually 10 pounds, at prices sometimes lower than paint stores. If you use a lot of rags, it pays to buy them in bulk.

Cheesecloth I use very fine cheesecloth purchased at a fabric store warehouse in a one-hundred yard box. The kind sold in paint stores is for straining paint and the weave is too open. Cheesecloth is excellent for softening painted areas, especially edges, more subtly than with rags.

Garbage bags Always have at least one plastic garbage bag on hand for trash.

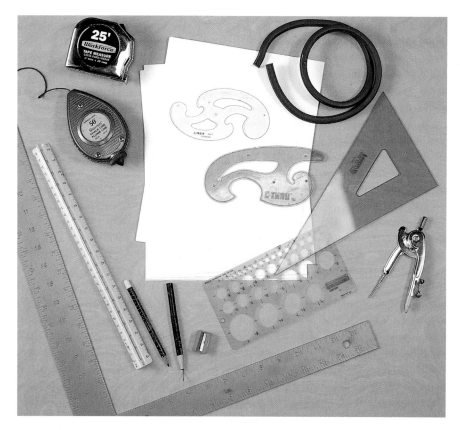

Miscellaneous drawing supplies include French curves, watercolor paper, templates, a compass, an architect's ruler, a lead pencil and sharpener, a grease pencil, a carpenter's square, triangles, a string line and a measuring tape.

Drawing Materials

Charcoal This is indispensable for laying out or transferring sketches (see *Transferring the Design* on page 28 for details).

Pencils It's good to have a few drawing pencils on hand in a range from soft to hard for making thumbnail sketches or helping with mural details.

Level Besides helping to make level or straight lines, this tool makes a great straightedge. Newer plastic levels are fairly inexpensive and lightweight.

Tracing paper It can be purchased in pads of various sizes or in large rolls (see *Transferring the Design*).

Overhead projector Use this for projecting images onto the walls, especially in large scale. Images, whether drawn, printed or photographed, must first be made into transparencies, a special film available for copy machines.

Opaque projectors allow you to project images directly from photos or drawings, but they require a much darker room.

Carpenter's square, triangles, circle templates, French curves, rulers, tape measure All of these are useful tools to help with the mural layout.

String line On occasion I use a carpenter's chalk line, filled with powdered artist's charcoal instead of chalk, to make long lines, especially perspective lines. If you are working alone, simply tape the end to the wall with blue tape, extend the string to the right point and snap the line, leaving a charcoal impression on the wall.

Erasers You will need these for erasing pencil lines, which are always hard to erase. That is why I use very little or no pencil. They can also be used to erase charcoal lines. My favorite is the Staedtler Mars plastic eraser, which is white and comes wrapped in paper.

Painting Materials

Brushes Painting murals on walls is tough on brushes, therefore, I avoid using overly expensive brushes. Among my favorite brushes are the Shipmate china bristle brushes by Elder and Jenks. They are relatively inexpensive but well made and unbelievably tough. And even though bristle brushes are made for oil paint, I have been using these brushes with water-based paints for years with great results. For finer work, I rely on nylon brushes. Loew-Cornell has a complete line of well-made brushes. For oil painting, I use these brushes and standard artist's bristle brushes. When using water mediums, avoid letting the paint dry out on your brushes. You want them to stay moist, but you also don't

A sealable palette (the Masterson brand is widely available) and a spray bottle filled with water are indispensable tools for water-based work.

want to leave them soaking in water. Rinse them frequently in clean water and lay them on the palette, or wrap them in a dampened rag or plastic temporarily (during lunch breaks, for example). Oil painting is less of a problem because the paint dries so slowly. To clean brushes, always wipe off the excess paint first and then rinse well in the appropriate solvent (water or thinner). Then lather them with either a mild soap or a special brush cleaner (such as the wonderful Masters brand), scrub into your palm, and repeat until the warm tap water runs clear through the bristles and the brush feels "squeaky" clean (see page 31).

Paint All of the projects in this book were done with acrylics or a combination of acrylics and commercial latex paint. For this reason, we will concern ourselves with water-based paints, although I do use oils. (Some of the murals shown in the Gallery on page 126 were executed in oils.) I use Golden acrylics because I believe they are the best commercially available paints. There are many less expensive brands, but as with oil paints, cheaper brands mean cheaper materials—inferior pigments, more fillers. Basically, you get what you pay for and cheaper colors are less brilliant, less clear and harder to blend.

Paints are basically finely-ground pigments suspended in a binding agent. For oil-based paints, this is an oil, usually linseed or safflower, and for water-based paints, it is a vinyl or acrylic-based resin. Common house paints are not manufactured for artistic use and therefore contain additives to increase their usability and shelf-life. However, these paints have improved dramatically over the years and many muralists use them because they are relatively inexpensive (a quart of latex is about the price of a small tube of good acrylic paint), readily available and easy to use. The problem with commercial latex paints is durability or longevity. Now, murals are not painted to last forever, but as an artist who strives to create something first rate and highly valued, I always like to believe that

Various-sized artist's brushes from different manufacturers, including flats and rounds.

A collection of various-sized artist's brushes from Loew-Cornell, including flats and rounds.

A collection of Shipmate china bristle brushes by Elder and Jenks.

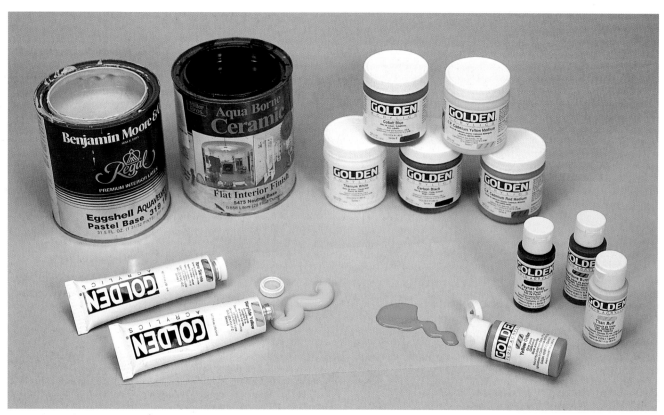

A collection of paints includes Benjamin Moore's Eggshell Acrylic and Miller Brothers' *Aqua Borne* Ceramic and a selection of Golden Acrylics.

my murals will be around for some time. In Italy, for instance, murals five or six centuries old are everywhere—an enriching and intimate part of the culture. In our contemporary, media-rich environment, we have become used to visual art that appears and disappears quickly. Permanence is something that each artist must consider for herself. If you choose to use commercial latex, then use the better brands. Even in this market, the better paints use better pigments and resins and fewer fillers. Also, remember that latex paints are more susceptible to moisture problems existing within walls. They are more porous (hence, allowing the wall to "breathe") than oils but are less resistant to moisture than artist's acrylics. Generally, however, from my own and others' experience, wall murals painted with latex paints hold up surprisingly well as long as the paint film is

not too watery thin or too thick.

Though not suggested or encouraged by manufacturers, latex and acrylic paints seem compatible enough. Often when using my acrylics, I substitute a latex white for the Titanium-Zinc White acrylic mixture that I usually use. I do this to increase coverage and opacity. At other times, I rough in the initial layers of a mural with latex, but complete the mural with acrylics. Occasionally, I have roughed in the initial layers with acrylics and then completed the mural with artist's oils. All of this depends on the size and extenuating circumstances of a particular job.

Water-based paints mostly lack the strong odor associated with oil-based paints and water is certainly more benign than paint thinner. Still, you need to be cautious with water-based paints as well. Latex paints exude fumes that

can be harmful in poorly ventilated areas and certain pigments—the cadmiums for example—are toxic if inhaled, regardless of whether they are ground in oil or acrylic resin. Common sense should be used. I recommend using a barrier cream on your hands. This is something like hand lotion that seals the pores and generally prevents paints from penetrating the skin. It washes off easily. Some art material companies make this product but it is often overpriced. Avon makes the best on the market—*Silicone Glove* hand cream—it actually softens your skin as well as protects it. Latex gloves are good to have on hand as well, although some people are allergic to them. They are best for really messy painting. Sometimes, however, they can be a bit cumbersome.

THEORY & PRACTICE

chapter 3

PERSPECTIVE: A BRIEF LESSON

Perspective is one of the primary tools that allows us to translate three-dimensional space and form onto a two-dimensional surface. There are many excellent books available on learning perspective and I encourage you to seek them out. Let's take a look at the basics.

Perspective reflects our visual experience of the world, most notably the way in which objects appear to diminish in size as they recede from us towards the horizon—the line marking the juncture of land and sky. These receding objects also become increasingly paler and bluer as the atmosphere's effect on them increases with their distance from us. Moreover, they become less clear, more blurred to our vision. This way in which the atmosphere affects visual phenomena, relative to spatial distances, is called atmospheric perspective. In landscape painting this translates into changes in value, color, and contrast as things recede in space: everything becomes bluer, lighter, more blurred. In contrast, however, the sky and clouds actually become warmer as they recede because they merge with the light and atmosphere of the warmer ground.

Understanding perspective begins with the concept of the picture plane, the imaginary flat surface onto which you transfer images. The picture plane is like a window held up before the world. (See illustration 1 on page 24.) The horizon—upon entering the picture plane—becomes the horizon line. The ground plane—the ground of the landscape—becomes the ground line at the base of the picture plane. (See illustration 2 on page 24.)

The surface area of a mural is the picture plane. Where the mural ends at the bottom, whether at the floor or at the baseboard, becomes the ground plane. So, this much is already established. Your first step, then, is to draw the horizon line. Most murals use a

Add a little Naples Yellow or Raw Sienna to your sky and clouds as they approach the horizon line. The sky gets bluer as it ascends and a bit greener as it descends. Clouds will be whiter/cooler on top and darker/warmer on the bottom as they ascend and warmer on top and cooler on the bottom (with less overall contrast) as they descend towards the horizon.

height of about 5 feet from the floor, which is the the viewer's eye level. Use a level to establish this line and draw it lightly with very soft charcoal (For studio renderings use a T-square).

For one-point perspective—meaning that all perspective lines converge in a single point on the horizon—you will next establish this single point, a vanishing point, somewhere along the horizon line. In this case we'll choose the center. (See illustration 3, below.)

Illustration 4 shows how parallel lines converge as they recede in this system. Objects placed here follow the same perspective rules. Adding recognizable imagery helps to show how this relates to the visual world (see illustration 5). In one-point perspective, objects are parallel to the picture plane. The cubes in illustration 6 show this clearly: notice how the top and bottom lines of the sides closest to us are parallel to the horizon and ground lines. The lines marking their sides follow the perspective lines towards the single, centered vanishing point.

For two-point perspective, all perspective lines converge in two vanishing points, rather than one. Often, these vanishing points are actually outside of the picture plane. Illustration 7 shows how, in two-point perspective, objects are no longer parallel to the picture plane. Their sides now recede either towards the left- or right-side vanishing points.

Illustration 8 shows how this translates into recognizable imagery.

Illustrations 9 & 10 show how to find the center of a side-plane in two-point perspective. The dotted line shows how this is useful for drawing circles in perspective.

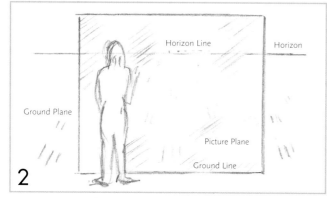

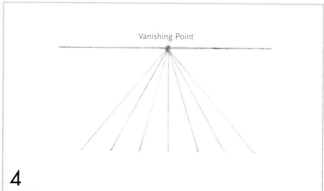

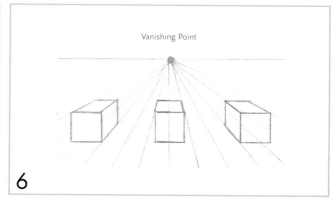

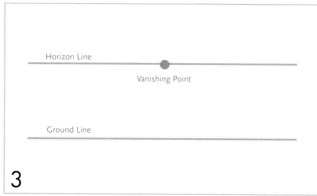

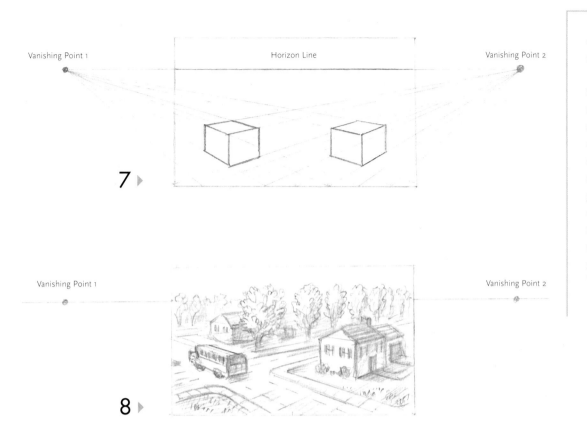

Vanishing Point 1   Horizon Line   Vanishing Point 2

7 ▶

Sometimes you may have to "fudge it," as they say, and make the perspective look right, regardless of the position of the vanishing points. This is especially true when turning corners. Don't worry about it! Trust your eyes.

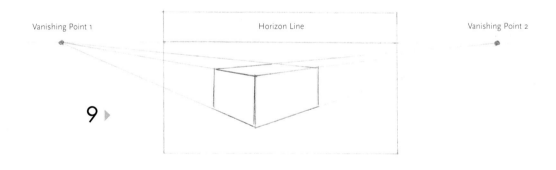

Vanishing Point 1   Vanishing Point 2

8 ▶

Vanishing Point 1   Horizon Line   Vanishing Point 2

9 ▶

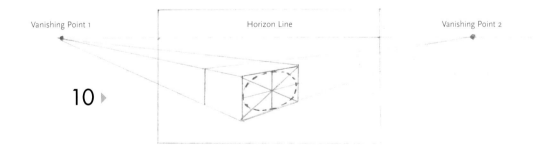

Vanishing Point 1   Horizon Line   Vanishing Point 2

10 ▶

COLOR

Color theory is a science unto itself, and it is an amazing and sometimes perplexing part of working with paints. I have painted for decades and still I am often surprised, delighted, and even sometimes frustrated by the limitless possibilities of color. Perhaps more than any other aspect of mural painting, using color requires hands-on experience. You have to observe the various pigments as they appear fresh out of their containers and how they look when intermixed in endless combinations.

Hue is the name given to a particular color, like "red." Familiarity with the color wheel (opposite) will help in understanding the families of color and how they relate to each other. Red, yellow and blue are the primary colors. They are the triangular foundation of the color wheel and, theoretically, you can mix all other colors from them. The next three colors on the wheel result from intermixing the primary colors: red + yellow to make

Remember that the same color will vary from one manufacturer to another and cheaper paints will have weaker color and less tinting strength.

orange; yellow + blue to make green; blue + red to make violet. These are the secondary colors. Each secondary color has a special relationship with a primary color and you will notice this relationship on the color wheel: each primary color is placed directly across from a secondary color; they are complementary colors. Red complements green; violet complements yellow; orange complements blue. This is important: you can soften the intensity of (or gray) a color by adding its complement, instead of adding black or white. You can also mix grays that are more vibrant than black/white mixtures. This idea of complementary color extends to many other non-primary colors. For example, I sometimes add ultramarine blue to burnt umber to gray it up a bit. Burnt Umber is not orange but, of the three secondary colors, it corresponds closest to orange. Quinacridone Crimson and Pthalo Green make a tremendous black color as well as gray; they are not the true primaries, but they are a red and a green: complementary colors (see illustration below).

Another important use for complementary colors is in shading. For example, if

5-Scale Value Chart

you're painting a yellow flower and want to shade it, adding black will darken it but will also possibly kill the color, making it greenish. Adding violet—yellow's complement—will darken it in a way that keeps the color lively.

White and black are not considered true colors and their use in painting relates to their ability to alter the value, or relative lightness or darkness, of colors. White added to a color is called a *tint*; black added to a color is called a *shade*; gray added to a color is called a *tone*.

Value and color are intimately related. When you mix a color, you must simultaneously be aware of the color's value. Limiting the value range at first may help you to deal with this issue. The illustration above shows a five-scale value chart: black, dark gray, medium gray, light gray, and white. If you can master the use of this limited scale, both in black and white and in color,

Have a non-absorbent sheet of paper or paperboard nearby on which to test your colors. For water-based paints, also have a hair dryer ready to dry the samples, as these paints dry darker. Labeling your mixes can save time later.

then you'll be in good shape to progress toward a broader understanding of value and color.

Colors are often characterized by their relative warmth or coolness, which connects them to the color wheel. The illustration on page 28 shows the basic separation of warm and cool colors. We tend to associate colors with temperature: yellow, orange, and red with the sun

Gray Mixtures

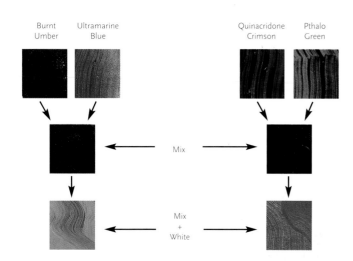

Burnt Umber · Ultramarine Blue

Quinacridone Crimson · Pthalo Green

Mix

Mix + White

or with fire; blue with the cold sky or with ice. Colors also have psychological connotations: red with anger, green with calm, blue with sadness. Bright colors grab our attention while dull colors tend to escape our notice. Conversely, too many bright colors can overwhelm us and duller colors can often soothe our tired eyes.

The illustration below presents an easy way to place colors on the palette and keep them separated according to their relative position on the color wheel. Earth colors, though mostly warm, are best kept to themselves, as are black and white.

The illustration on page 29 shows the five components of light upon an object. For most applications, this translates simply to the notion of warm and cool colors: highlights are cool; lights are warm; shadows are cool; reflected light is warm; cast shadows are cool. This is simplified, of course, but it helps greatly for blocking in or underpainting. Notice how warm and cool alternate.

Color Wheel

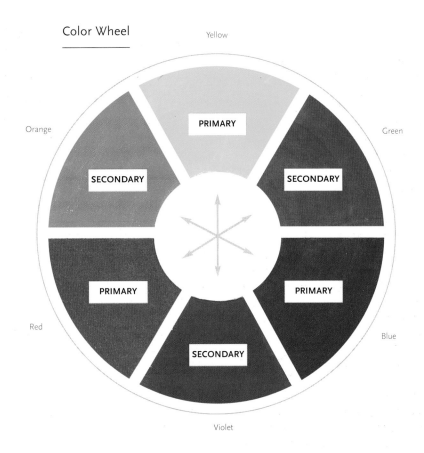

Color Arrangement on the Palette

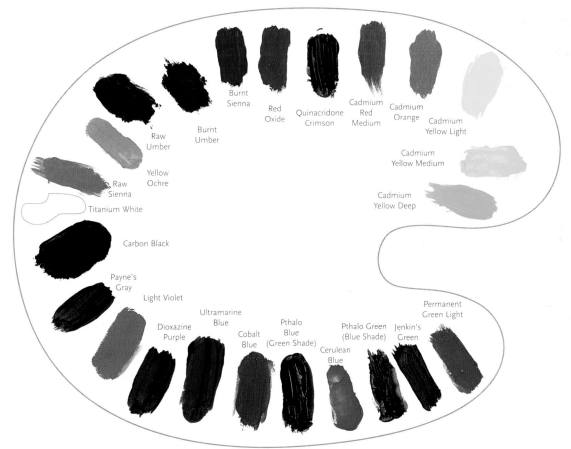

Cool/Warm Color Wheel

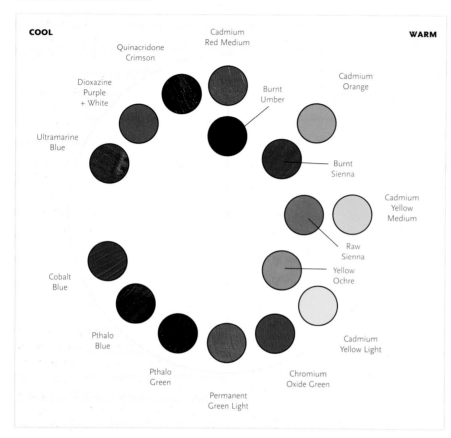

COOL   **WARM**

Quinacridone Crimson

Cadmium Red Medium

Dioxazine Purple + White

Burnt Umber

Cadmium Orange

Ultramarine Blue

Burnt Sienna

Cadmium Yellow Medium

Raw Sienna

Cobalt Blue

Yellow Ochre

Pthalo Blue

Cadmium Yellow Light

Pthalo Green

Chromium Oxide Green

Permanent Green Light

TRANSFERRING THE DESIGN

Projection

An overhead projector often provides an easy method for transferring certain images to a larger, vertical surface. This requires converting the image to be transferred onto a transparency, which is a clear plastic film. You can get this done at many commercial copy centers for a small fee. An opaque projector allows you to project images directly from the source, but it requires a much darker working space; hence, the advantage of the overhead projector, which works in most light conditions. Slide projectors are more familiar to most of us and they can be handy to project slides, but they also need a darkened room to be effective.

Tracing Paper Transfer

My primary method of transferring images to walls is an extremely simple one. Basically, it involves placing tracing paper on top of the image to be copied and tracing the outline of the image onto the paper's surface. Then this outline is traced on the reverse side with medium or soft charcoal. I mostly use stick instead of pencil charcoal because it seems to transfer better. In the next step, the tracing paper is held in place on the wall (using safe-release white tape if needed). With the charcoal side against the wall, rub sufficiently to transfer the charcoal onto the wall (see the Tuscan Landscape and Clouds projects—pages 38 & 78).

Another (very old) method begins after the image is either drawn or transferred onto sturdy drawing paper. Trace the outline, using a pounce wheel, which cuts tiny holes along the outline. Next, the paper is held in place and a powder is rubbed over the lines. I use powdered charcoal; others prefer powdered chalk. This transfers a dotted line onto the surface.

Scaling

This method uses grid lines to copy a drawing or outline. The grid placed over the original must be proportionally scaled to the grid placed on the final surface. (If you don't want to put lines on your drawing, you can put them on tracing paper laid on top of the drawing.) For example, the original grid might have half-inch (12mm) squares and the copy grid might have five-inch (127mm) squares; therefore, the mural drawing will be ten times larger than the original drawing (10 x 1/2" [12mm] = 5" [127mm]). The idea is to copy the lines exactly as they appear in each square, enlarging accordingly.

Freehand

It takes a certain amount of confidence to transfer a design onto a wall completely freehand—or with no mechanical aids. You need to be sensitive to proportions, to relationships between elements within the drawing and to the edges of the picture plane (the flat surface area encompassing the mural). Nevertheless, the best way to gain that confidence is to simply do it. When drawing with soft charcoal, mistakes can easily be erased or covered over. Never sketch a mural with pencil or other hard media as covering the lines will be difficult. I use vine charcoal when I want only a shadow of a line left after dusting off the excess charcoal, and willow charcoal when I want a darker line.

Be aware that a design that works well on a small sheet of drawing paper will not automatically work on a large wall. Draw the design with your eyes keenly focused on the space before you—on the boundaries of that space and the rhythms and spatial relationships

Always step back as far as possible and spend some time looking at and analyzing your design—letting your vision move occasionally to the mural's surroundings—to make sure that everything works together.

between the elements being drawn rather than being too narrowly focused on the source material. This helps to breathe life and harmony into your composition.

The illustration to the right shows the five components of light upon an object: highlight, light, shadow, reflected light and cast shadow. If you can master this concept (keeping in mind that the edges of forms must be softened to show that they are turning away from us), then you will be able to render any three-dimensional form convincingly. Notice that the direction from which the light comes is clearly shown. Also, notice how the reflected light begins exactly where the cast shadow ends. This dark background is essential. Where the background moves into light, there is no longer a surface close enough from which light can bounce back into the shadowed part of the object.

ROUGHING IN THE DESIGN

How to Cover Broad Areas

Painting a very large mural can be a daunting task if you're not used to it. The best advice I can give is to approach the mural broadly at first. Do not allow yourself to start painting details until the entire surface is blocked in—that is, until you have at least either a wash or a basic layer of paint over the entire surface. This wash may be a watercolor. It doesn't matter as long as you are giving attention to every element of your design. Many muralists use commercial latex because it covers large areas more easily and costs much less. As I mentioned earlier, I sometimes add latex white to the mix in order to cover better. And I have done entire murals in latex. I've also done very large projects entirely with artist's acrylics because the colors are richer.

I use the large Shipmate brushes—3.5-inch (89mm) and 4-inch (102 mm)—to cover large areas, often scrubbing the paint on as well as brushing it on. On

Five Components of Light Upon an Object

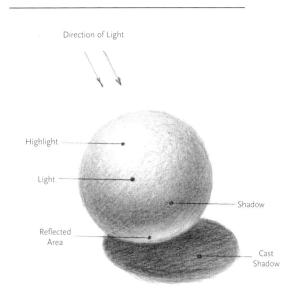

Direction of Light

Highlight

Light

Shadow

Reflected Area

Cast Shadow

As with most drawing endeavors, it helps to move your entire arm as you sketch on the wall. Draw with your elbow and shoulder in play, not just your wrist. This helps give liveliness and rhythm to your line.

rare occasions, I will use a small roller to apply the paint, but will then quickly brush it out or otherwise texture it with a cotton rag or cheesecloth.

You can also wipe the surface with a dampened rag to allow the large brush to move more easily, but you have to be careful not to get the wall too damp as the paint will run and/or not adhere well. If you are using an acrylic glaze medium, you can get a glaze medium/water mix for this purpose.

Monochromatic Base

Roughing in your design over large areas can also be made easier by limiting your palette at first. I ordinarily do this in two ways. First, I use only a few earth colors, like Raw Sienna, Burnt Sienna and Raw Umber (with black added for darker values) and wipe off with a rag for highlights. Second, I use the five-value gray scale—black, white and either three values mixed with these two or three values of other mixed grays, like Burnt Umber and Ultramarine Blue or Pthalo Green and Quinacridone Crimson.

The entire composition is blocked in with this monochromatic underpainting, allowing you to concentrate on drawing, values and design. Final colors are layered on top, or glazes can be brushed on for a final effect or as an intermediate step for further painting.

Contrasting Colors

This is simply underpainting in a color that is either opposite the final color on the color wheel or is contrasted in terms of warm versus cool. I often underpaint foliage in very reddish earth tones (even mixing red in with Burnt Sienna) before proceeding with the greenish mixes (see the Tuscan Landscape project).

Varnishing

Unlike oil colors, the paint film made with acrylics is flexible and porous, meaning that it allows moisture to pass through from within. It is also water-resistant, allowing for a mild cleaning with soap and water. It does not require varnishing, which is the application of a protective film. Nevertheless, many clients request varnishing and many locations demand extra protection. Using artist's varnish, which comes in tiny bottles, would be prohibitively expensive. Instead, I use commercial latex varnish. The best I've found so far is Pratt and Lambert's Acrylic Latex Varnish, available in dull, satin and gloss sheens, which can be intermixed. This must be applied quickly but carefully with a paint roller and 3/8-inch (10mm) roller cover after cutting in edges first with a nylon brush (the same procedure for painting walls with latex). It is advisable to wear a respirator.

BASIC PAINTING TECHNIQUES

chapter 4

There are certain painting techniques you will need to familiarize yourself with if you are interested in being a muralist. I have put together a few of the most common elements encountered in mural painting and I have demonstrated techniques required to paint them in this chapter. Also, I have touched upon several organizational and general pointers which will ensure that your painting will be successful and as fuss-free as possible.

This is a Masterson Sta–Wet Palette. It's a great tool for ensuring that your paint doesn't dry out while you're painting.

Here, I'm showing how to test the wall paint to see if it's latex or oil. Rub a bit of rubbing alcohol on the wall. If the paint comes off, as it did in this picture, the wall has been painted with latex (water–based) paint.

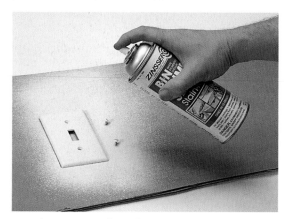

Don't forget to spray the outlet covers and switchplates with BIN primer and then carefully brush on the same base paint that you use for the rest of the wall. When you paint a mural, your canvas is the entire wall.

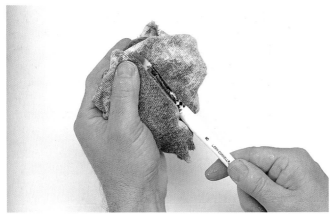

1 When cleaning your brush, first wipe off all excess paint with a cloth.

2 Then rinse your brush (assuming you have been using acrylic paints) in clean water.

3 Next, apply brush cleaner to your bristles.

4 Stroke the bristles back and forth in your hand to really work the brush cleaner product into your brush bristles.

5 Then, form the bristles into the shape they were when the brush was first purchased.

Wrap up your cleaned brushes in a clean rag.

Then, put the bundled-up brushes in a plastic bag.

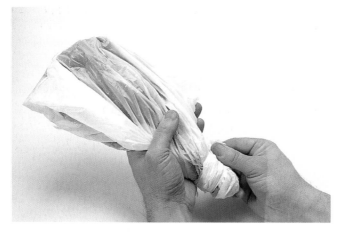

Either knot the end of the bag as shown or use a Ziploc bag to make the bag airtight.

Store your leftover paint in (from left to right) a generic tin paint can purchased at a homegoods store, a disposable plastic container with a cover, or a heavier-gauge plastic storage container.

If you're using a plastic container, put quick-release tape around the lid to form a better seal. Remember to date and label the paint.

TREE COLORS

A

B

C

D

▲ **1** Sketch in the basic outline of where you want the trees to be with a no. 4 round and tree color A. If you have trunk parts, you can go right over them in order to darken them.

▲ **2** With the same color and a 1-inch (25mm) flat brush, paint in the foliage. You must think about the direction in which the foliage is growing. Push the brush in that direction and think about the form of the tree in order to give it depth.

▲ **3** Next, add some glaze medium to tree color B for a little transparency and add more foliage to the treetops. Don't cover up too much. You want to be sure to get the luminescence—the play between the cooler green and the warmer reddish brown—especially in the shadow areas and reflected light areas.

▲ **4** With a 1-inch (25mm) flat brush loaded with color C, tap lightly on a dry rag to make sure you don't have too much color on the brush. Using the dry-brush technique with a very light touch, follow the contours of the trees, accentuating the light source, which is coming from the upper left here.

◄ **5** With color D on your 1-inch (25mm) flat, add more highlights in the same manner. Change to a no. 4 round and sparingly add detail leaves. This brings the trees a little closer to your eyes and gives them a little more rhythm. In darker areas, you can just put dots to suggest leaves and to break up the color.

STONE COLORS

E

F

G

H

I

J

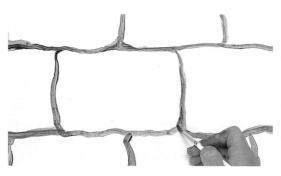

▲ **1** With a no. 4 round stain brush loaded with color E, get the basic outline of the stones just so you know where you're going.

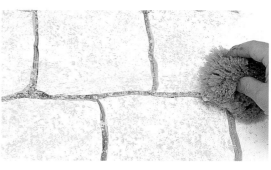

▲ **2** Wet a sea sponge and wring it out really well and apply colors F and G. Try not to make it look too regular. You want a mottled look here.

▲ **3** With a touch of glaze and color H on a 2-inch (51mm) bristle brush, stipple and smash the brush around in order to "scrub" in the color.

▲ **4** Now take your sponge and stipple in color I.

▲ **5** Reline the lines with a no. 4 round stain brush loaded with color E. Think in terms of light coming from above. Also, add little holes in the stone.

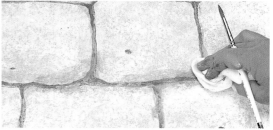

▲ **6** Using your no. 4 round stain brush, thin color E with a little water and use this same color for the shadow. Blot with a cheesecloth.

▲ **7** Using your no. 4 round stain brush loaded with color J, make the top lip of the stone a bit thicker and use color I on the holes to add highlights.

GRASS COLORS

K

L

M

N

▲ **1** With a 2-inch (51mm) bristle brush loaded with color K and Aquaglaze, start at the top with the smallest strokes and go toward the bottom with bigger strokes, where the perspective is nearest the viewer. As you're working, pull toward yourself with short strokes. As you get close to the foreground, you can also push away from yourself.

▲ **2** With your 2-inch (51mm) bristle brush loaded with color L thinned with Aquaglaze, push and stipple the color from top to bottom, making the color thicker at the bottom.

To speed up drying time, you may want to use a hair dryer after the second step. If it's not dry enough, the next layer will pull off what's underneath.

Occasionally, add horizontal strokes to break up the vertical strokes. That way, all the strokes won't be going in the same direction.

Use some of the sky color as a glaze to push back the top of the grassy field at the horizon line.

▲ **3** Load your no. 4 round brush with color M and paint individual blades of grass—bigger in the foreground and smaller in the background.

▲ **4** Now, using your no. 2 round brush loaded with color N, paint more blades of grass here and there in this highlight color.

TRUNK COLORS

P

Q

R

S

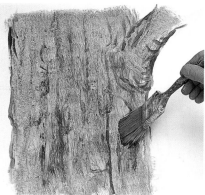

◀ **1** *(Left)* With a no. 4 round stain brush loaded with color P, cartoon in the basic shape of a tree trunk and bark.

◀ **2** *(Right)* Load your 2 1/2-inch (64mm) bristle brush with color P and watered-down glaze medium and scrub in the color, stippling and pushing in the side of the brush in a *frottage* technique.

◀ **3** *(Left)* With your no. 4 round brush loaded with color P, add more bark, making most of the contrast in the middle and getting rid of the contrast toward the edges.

◀ **4** *(Right)* Use your 2 1/2-inch (64mm) bristle brush and color Q and stipple in gray. Use more on the sides.

◀ **5** *(Left)* Put lines back in with color R loaded on your no. 4 round brush.

◀ **6** *(Right)* Highlight now with your no. 8 flat stain brush loaded with color S.

Re-use some of the gray glaze to push elements back away from your eye.

◀ **7** Put lines back in with R loaded on your no. 4 round brush.

WATER/SKY COLORS

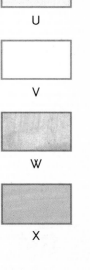

U

V

W

X

▲ **1** To create the sky, first apply a mix of water + glaze to the surface.

▲ **2** With color U loaded on your 3-inch (76mm) bristle brush, coat the surface.

▲ **3** With that same brush loaded with colors U and W, use the wet-on-wet technique and fill in the top of the sky.

▲ **4** With your no. 8 flat stain brush loaded with color V, put in stratus clouds. Go over with Titanium White. Add a little more V at the horizon.

▲ **5** For the water, repeat steps 1 through 4 and then add color X near the land mass.

▲ **6** When doing the reflection, take the image—in this case, the house—and make an upside-down version with glaze + water. Then, with a dry, soft brush, brush over it to smear it a bit. Make sure the reflected image is less defined and has fewer details. Using color V, put streaks in the water.

TUSCAN LANDSCAPE

project 1

Landscapes work wonderfully in many different kinds of rooms. They open up the space visually and give a wonderful comforting sensibility to interiors. Though they need to be composed, they can allow more painterly freedom than architectural views or representations of people or animals. This client wanted a landscape that would work within a particular color scheme and the Tuscan landscape helps in that regard. I composed it to recognize the long wall and partial cathedral ceiling. The column on the left and the drape on the right work almost like bookends, framing the whole mural. Adding elements like the road at the right and the receding red flowers helps to create convincing space.

COLOR CHART

Throughout this project, the colors used will be indicated by the letters shown here.

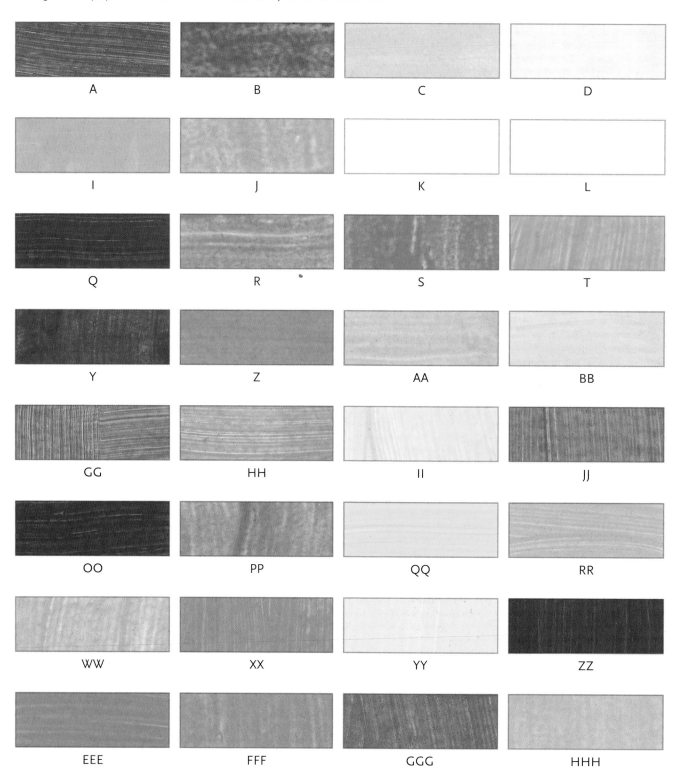

A	B	C	D
I	J	K	L
Q	R	S	T
Y	Z	AA	BB
GG	HH	II	JJ
OO	PP	QQ	RR
WW	XX	YY	ZZ
EEE	FFF	GGG	HHH

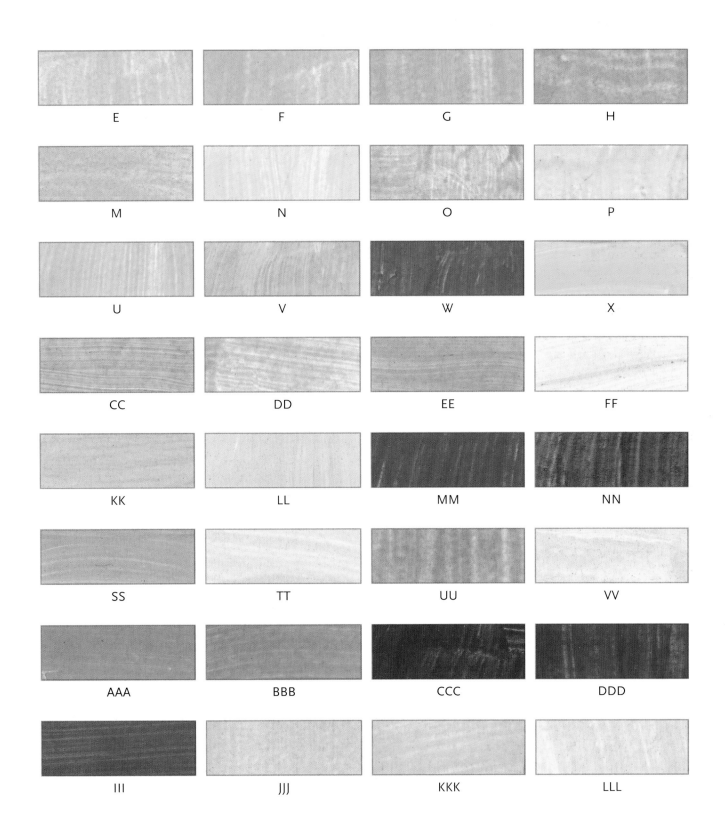

E

F

G

H

M

N

O

P

U

V

W

X

CC

DD

EE

FF

KK

LL

MM

NN

SS

TT

UU

VV

AAA

BBB

CCC

DDD

III

JJJ

KKK

LLL

▲ **1** Prepare your room. Use quick-release tape to protect the woodwork from the wall surface and be sure to use plastic sheeting and drop cloths on the floor.

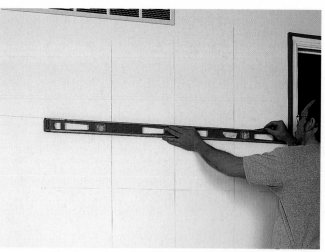

▲ **2** Square up your wall surface into a grid pattern.

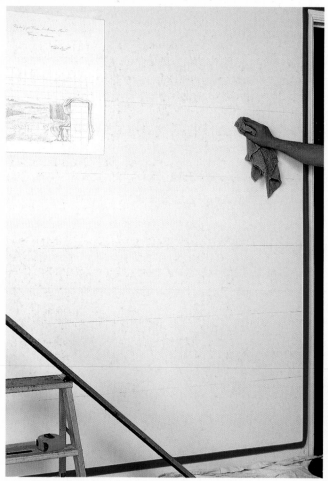

▲ **3** Oops! I didn't respect the rendering's squaring. I came out with a whole square next to the right-hand door frame and the rendering only has half a square. Now I have to redo it. It's easier to redo the wall markings than it would be to redo the rendering!

▲ **4** Sketch in the outline of the design using the squared-off rendering as the pattern.

▲ **5** This is the incorrect way to turn a corner. When you try to make things work, especially when you are up close (on a ladder, for example), it looks correct to you. You really need to move back to get the true perspective.

▲ **6** This is the correct way to turn a corner. Make sure there's not a "V" angle in the corner.

▲ **7** Here you have the entire penciled-in design in a triptych of photos. In the middle one, I am "spanking" the wall or pouncing a cloth on the wall to lightly dust off the charcoal grid, leaving a very light tracing so you can barely see it.

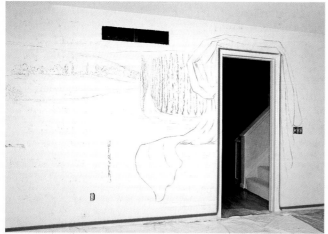

8 *(Above and Right)* Italians call this stage *cartooning*. Use a no. 6 round brush loaded with A and go over the charcoaled lines of the design. I'm not cartooning in some of the balustrade and stonework because it'll be easier to wash it in first and then to work around it.

9 You can use a liner brush with a straightedge for architectural details such as this column.

◀ **10** With a 2- or 3-inch (51 or 76mm) bristle brush loaded with B + a little glaze, lay in the wash. So that the color is not too uniform, take your brush and pounce in the color, literally crushing the brush into the wall. That way you will achieve a mottled effect. I often do this step first as an *imprimatura* and put the lines of my design in afterwards. Here, I'm doing the opposite.

▼ **11** Take a damp rag and wipe off any excess wash. You want this wash to be very subtle.

Cartooning your mural means simply that you are drawing the basic design onto the wall, concerned mostly with composition and other technical details, like proportion, perspective, and style. The drawn outlines can be as precise or as sketchy as you like.

Laying in the wash is adding the element of value to the line drawing (or cartoon). It doesn't have to be overly thought-out; rather, it should give some depth to the cartoon and help you to begin visualizing what the final mural will look like.

The imprimatura does a similar job, but it is washed in all over the surface before the cartooning and so does not follow any outlines of forms.

▲ **12** Using a no. 10 flat stain brush loaded with C, paint the hills, making them darker as they near the houses. On the left side where the light is coming from, use D with bigger strokes as you come down in an effort to lose the edge.

▲ **13** For the distant trees, pick up your no. 6 round brush and load it with E. Use F for the windows of the buildings and G for the chimney. Use H to paint the stones on the buildings.

▲ **14** Use your no. 10 flat stain brush and your no. 24 flat brush loaded with I and J for laying down the greens of the grassy hill, alternating between the warm and cool greens. Soften the edges of the mountains with K in order to make them appear more rounded. Pull the farthest hill back behind the other one with L.

▲ **15** *(Above left)* Now paint the field of harvested hay with M washed on and rubbed in with a 2-inch (51mm) brush. Make this as irregular as possible.

▲ **16** *(Above Right)* Soften the edge of the hill with N and then use O over the furrows to soften even further.

◀ **17** *(Bottom Left)* Load your brush with P and using broad strokes, pounce in order to give grasslike structure to the lower hill.

▲ **18** In order to create the woods, take a 2-inch (51mm) brush loaded with Q and scrub the color on to the left and to the right. Use a back-and-forth motion to soften the lower areas. Use a stipple motion at top in order to round the treetops.

▲ **19** Use R for the foreground grassy field.

▲ **20** Highlight the trees in the woods with a 1-inch (25mm) brush loaded with S. Stipple the color in the way the leaves grow. Don't let your brushstrokes get too regular. Use your no. 6 round brush to detail the leaves.

▲ **21** Now take T and U and detail more leaves. In order to give the illusion that the background is showing through, take a color that is similar to the background color—which in this case is V—and paint little breaks in the foliage.

▲ **22** Using W, put in blades of grass in the foreground field. Use an upward motion with your brush.

▲ **23** Pull through with your brush, using horizontal strokes to soften the effect.

▲ **24** Since you have W already loaded on your brush, go ahead and jump over to the cypress trees and base them in, using your no. 24 flat. Be sure to follow the movement of the leaves, which fan out in a left and right motion.

▲ **25** For the furrowed field, take X and dry-brush the color on. With your finger or palette knife, scrape the paint a bit to make it less even. Then go back with a no. 6 flat brush with more color and stipple over the top a bit to add in more color.

▲ **26** *(Above Left)* For the poppies, use a no. 6 filbert loaded with Y. Paint the foreground flowers first.

▲ **27** *(Above Right)* For the more distant flowers, use that same color on a no. 4 shader and blot color off the flowers farthest in the distance to approximate a drybrush technique.

▶ **28** *(Right)* Using a no. 6 round, highlight these flowers with Z.

▲ **29** For the safflowers, use a no. 6 round loaded with AA. Your flower blossoms can be very impressionistic—just daubs.

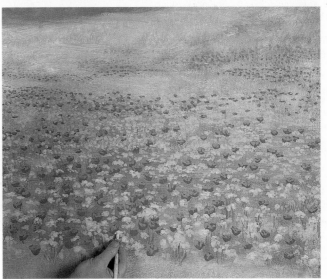

▲ **30** Highlight these flowers with BB.

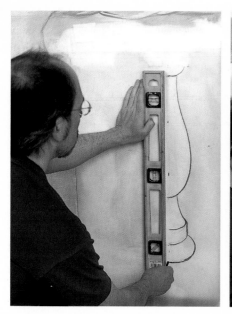

▲ **31** For the balustrade, tape up the tracing paper and square up the bottom and top rails with a level and yardstick. Then freehand one side of a baluster on the tracing paper.

▲ **32** Turn the tracing paper so that the charcoal side is facing the wall. Rub with charcoal so that the imprint is on the wall.

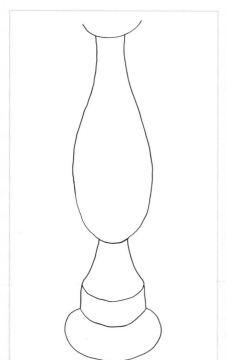

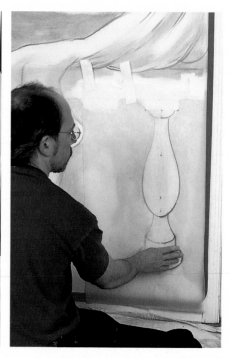

This pattern may be hand-traced or photocopied for personal use only. Enlarge at 200%, then 200% again, then at 171% to bring to full size.

▲ **33** Retrace the one side of the baluster on the outside of the tracing paper. Remember to trace the guidelines as well.

▲ **34** Turn the tracing paper around and rub.

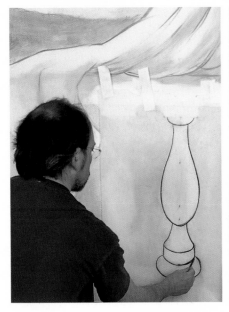

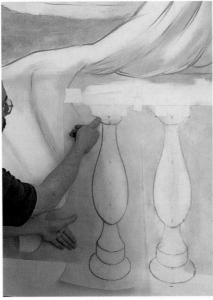

▲ **35** Now trace both sides of the baluster in order to have a symmetrical pattern to use on the rest of the balustrade.

▲ **36** Tape the tracing paper up for the second baluster next to the finished baluster.

▲ **37** Using a liner brush, outline the balustrade with CC. The charcoal will disappear under this color. In order to get the true center from one baluster to another, measure over from one center to the next, using your level to keep everything straight.

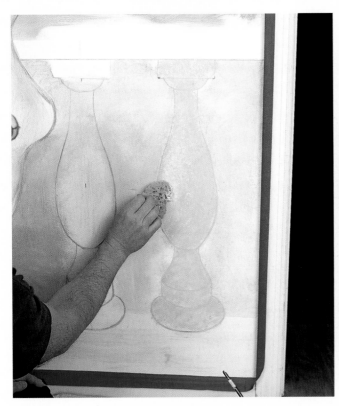

▲ **38** Next, apply a wash of DD over the entire inside of the baluster and add EE to the center of the element.

▲ **39** Paint FF on either side of the dark center part of the baluster with a sponge. Using GG, add shadows to the balustrade.

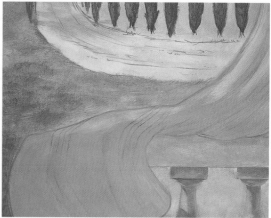

41 Charcoal in the stripes of the fabric, making sure to create a twist in the fabric.

40 For the drape around the framed doorway, load a 2-inch (51mm) brush with HH and tint the darker areas with a dry-brush technique. Then, with a 1-inch (25mm) brush and II, highlight the drape. Use a damp rag to wipe off paint in order to create highlights.

It helps to work with a real piece of fabric as you create these folds and twists, preferably a fabric similar to the one you are portraying in your mural.

42 Using your no. 4 liner loaded with KK, line the red stripes in the fabric. This pinstripe serves as a placeholder for the red stripe.

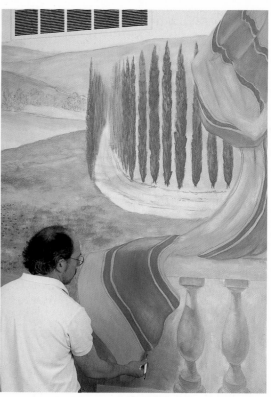

43 Next, block in the red parts of the stripes with JJ and the green parts with S. When making the stripes, you have to follow the line next to the one you are painting with your peripheral vision at the same time that you're watching the line you're actually painting. It's sort of like patting your head and rubbing your stomach at the same time!

You can correct any mistakes by using a damp rag wrapped around your finger. Take a damp piece of fine cheesecloth and wipe away color to suggest reflected light. If you need to add back color, do so once again with a dry-brush technique.

▲ **44** Base the column with KK and LL and then use the same colors and techniques to highlight and shade this element as with the balustrade. (See page 53.)

▲ **45** Detail the architectural elements with your no. 6 round. Use MM.

▲ **46** Next, add a little glaze to NN. Apply it with your no. 10 flat brush to the right side of the column and column base because of the way the light is entering the room. Smooth and soften with a wet rag as needed.

▲ **48** Continuing with your no. 10 flat, add cast shadows under the ivy with PP. This is a little touch that makes the mural more believable, especially since the natural light coming from the bank of windows to the left of the column is so harsh.

▲ **47** With your no. 10 flat loaded with OO, add ivy leaves around the column.

▲ **49** *(Top Left)* Add QQ and RR alternately to the middle ground light field. Notice that I changed the path of the road a bit. Not a problem. I just sketched right over the paint with charcoal. This is the version I decided to use.

▲ **50** *(Top Right)* Paint the hill where the distant road goes using SS. The road itself is TT. Add shadows on the left side of the hill with UU and add highlights to the right side of the hill with VV.

◄ **51** For the foreground road in between the cypress trees, use WW, putting it on thickly and then wiping it off to create a mottled effect.

◀ **52** *(Left)* Add ruts to the road with XX using a dry-brush technique.

◀ **53** *(Right)* Highlight the road area with YY and put first details on the trees with ZZ.

▲ **54** *(Above)* Create tree shadows on the road with AAA. It's important to establish where the light source is coming from. Here, I have established that the light is coming from the left and it's a late morning light. The shadows should be less visible as they go back. Also, there is a subtle cast shadow from the grass on the left side of the road. Drybrush BBB over any shadows that need to be warmed up. Then, wipe off with a cheesecloth if needed.

▶ **55** *(Right)* Next, highlight the cypress trees with your no. 6 round and EEE. Try to follow the way the branches grow and to make it look as though the light is coming from the left.

Use CCC on your no. 6 round and add brown to the tree trunks. Also, add DDD behind the cypress trees on the grass to establish the shadows there.

▲ **56** Charcoal in the shepherd's hut and sheep.

▲ **57** Block in the hut with your no. 6 round and 1/2-inch (12mm) flat loaded with FFF. Paint the roof with your no. 6 round and GGG. Use HHH for the sheep.

▲ **58** Add shadows to the door, windows and roof overhang with III. It's important here to create details without getting too distinct and strong. The hut is far away and can't stand out too much. For the stonework, use JJJ. Add shadows to the stone fence and dirt to the pen area with III. Highlight the sheep with K.

▲ **59** The field surrounding the hut looked too stark to me, so I added dirt patches and grass patches here and there with a 1/2-inch (12mm) flat loaded with KKK and LLL. Drybrush the color on and rub off with a piece of dampened cheesecloth. You can also use LLL to add highlights to the top of the stone hut.

◀ **60** Charcoal in the broken part of the balustrade rail.

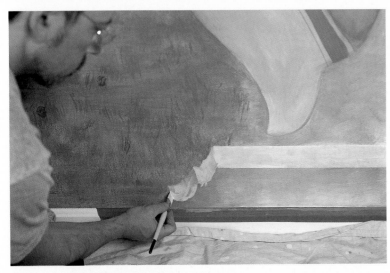

◀ **61** Scrub color onto the balustrade using the same colors as before. (See steps 37, 38 and 39 on page 53.) As you add the highlights and shadows, be sure to keep in mind the way the light would hit the balustrade.

◀ **62** Using a 3/4 inch (18mm) flat brush, add cracks with the dark value.

▲ **63** When using a *trompe l'oeil* element in your mural, you can enhance the "trickery" aspect by adding three-dimensional elements. Here I have added a simple tie-back to the drape element. This helps anchor the drape and balustrade in the foreground of the mural.

Place a hanger bolt in the wall where the curtain tieback would be and place a set of tassels on it.

▲ **64** Screw in the tieback. Here, I used a gold-leafed medallion.

Finished Mural

Above is the middle section of the finished mural. The photos to the right are the left and right sides surrounding the doorways.

MONKEY

project 2

This client had very specific ideas about what she wanted, so I didn't monkey around with the concept. I tried to make it believable, without being scary. The scariness usually is found in the face, so I concentrated on a realistic but somewhat friendly facial appearance. The monkey looks toward another mural: hence the client wanted it to scratch its head while contemplating the scene. The tail is carefully curved to create a rhythm suited to that corner space, relating to the curtain hardware and the adjacent grandfather clock.

Throughout this project, the colors used will be indicated by the letters shown here.

A

B

C

D

E

F

This pattern may be hand–traced or photo-copied for personal use only. Enlarge at 200%, and enlarge again at 179% to bring it up to full size.

G

H

I

J

K

L

M

N

▲ **1** After transferring the monkey design to the wall with transfer paper and charcoal, paint over the lines with color A, using a no. 6 round brush. This paint should be of a watercolor consistency, but not so thin as to run.

▲ **2** Using a no. 10 flat stain brush and the same color A, block in the monkey with thin washes. Add more water to the washes for the vest and face, so they appear lighter.

▲ **3** Use the no. 10 flat brush and color B to further wash in the face and define its form. This color should be thinned with a fair amount of water. Use a no. 6 round brush for smaller areas of the wash.

▲ **4** Use the no. 10 flat brush and color C to block in the vest and the darker values of the banana. Use the no. 6 round brush and color D to block in the rest of the banana.

▲ **5** Using the no. 6 round and colors E and A, add details to the monkey's fur. Let the movement of your brush follow the contours of the various body parts. It may help to start at the bottom and work upwards (on the leg, for example), to suggest overlapping fur. Color A is darker and will be used more towards the shadowed areas, where the form turns away from the light source. Next, use the same brush with colors F and G to paint highlights in the fur, including the face. Add enough water to give a sharp painted line. Then add the white fur around the face with the no. 6 round and colors G and H. Remember to move from darker to lighter values: A to E to F to G to H.

▲ **6** Continue to add details with the same colors. You may need to allow some dry time (or use a hairdryer) to get crisper details. Use color I for reflected light (e.g., underside of arms and thigh). Use a smaller brush if that makes it easier.

▲ **8** Use the no. 10 flat brush and color L to wash over the vest to enrich its color. With a no. 12 shader and color M, shadow the vest where it turns away from the viewer and light source. Use the same brush and color N to highlight the vest.

With a no. 4 round—an old brush, perhaps even a throwaway—apply gold size wherever you want to apply gold leaf. I use quick-dry synthetic Rollco 79 varnish. Wait until the size is tacky. It should "snap" when you lightly press your finger and quickly let go.

▲ **7** Using no. 6 and no. 4 round brushes, and color J, further heighten the banana peel and use color K to highlight the banana.

▲ **9** You're ready to apply gold leaf. The backing paper is gently held in place and then rubbed with a soft brush and/or fingers. Broken or tiny pieces of leaf can be over–laid to fill open spaces.

▲ **10** Continue to add leaf. You can always apply more size to other areas where you might want more leaf. Just remember to allow drying time until it's tacky.

The Completed Monkey

HOME THEATER

project 3

This client wanted a retro theater lobby painted in the hallway leading to their real—life home theater. The space was difficult—it was close to a stairwell. I composed it to be seen both by people descending the stairs as well as by those to the right and around the corner. The perspective had to work for all views, which is why the horizon line is a bit higher than usual. With limited colors in the surrounding space, I also limited my palette. I tried to make the space convincing but fun, and I added some period elements for a retro look.

Throughout this project, the colors used will be indicated by the letters shown here.

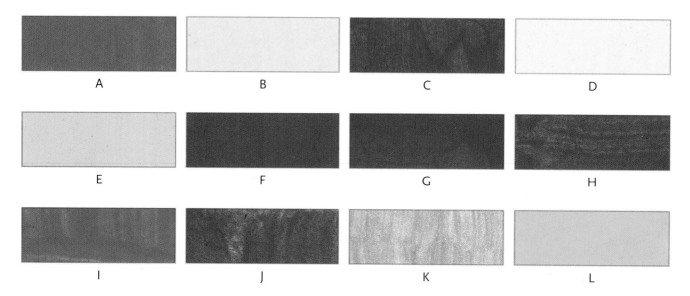

A

B

C

D

E

F

G

H

I

J

K

L

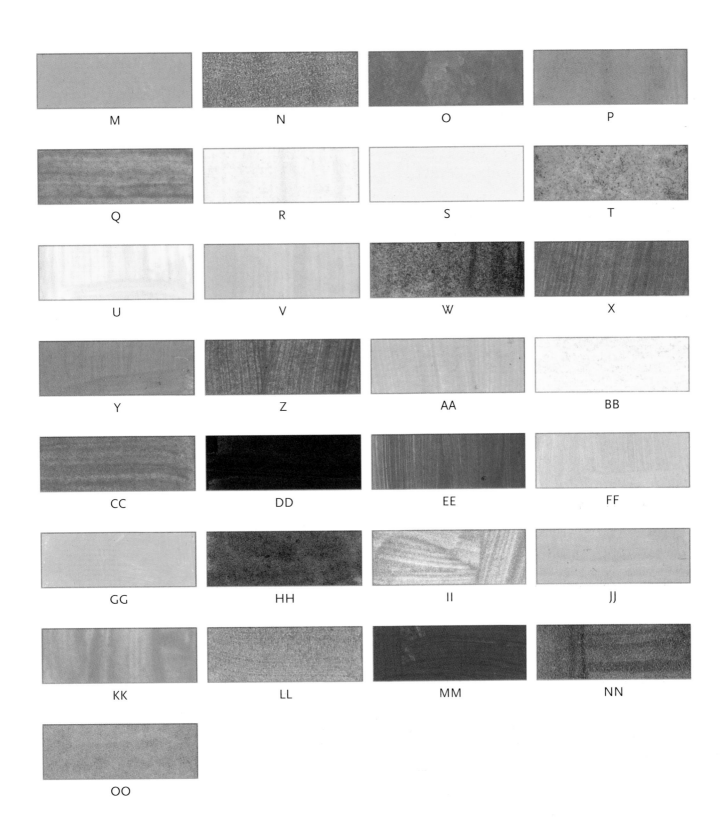

M

N

O

P

Q

R

S

T

U

V

W

X

Y

Z

AA

BB

CC

DD

EE

FF

GG

HH

II

JJ

KK

LL

MM

NN

OO

◄ 1 *(Left)* Sketch design on wall with charcoal and then go over it with a graphite pencil because of the architectural nature of the subject.

◄ 2 *(Right)* Wipe off the charcoal but make sure that you are still able to see the pencil marks

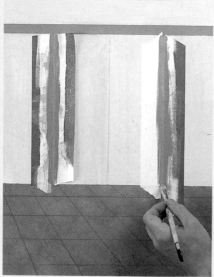

▲ 3 Block in the design with a 3/8-inch (10mm) roller and a 4-inch (96mm) flat brush. Use F for the floor and G for the foreground wall. When painting this wall, first paint the wall with a roller and then go back with the 4-inch (96mm) brush and stipple the paint, for a "faux" technique. Use C for the curved wall, E for the wall immediately behind the curved wall, B for the ceiling light, and A for the area around the light and the base for the poster on the right. Next, lay in the door with D and Titanium White. Then, take the flat surface of a rolled rag and pull vertically and pounce. Use cheesecloth to soften the effect.

▲ 4 With safe-release tape, tape off the larger partitions of the door frame., making sure the lines are straight. Darken the door frame with F. Use a liner brush with a straight edge in order to create the center door line.

▲ 5 With a level, mark the door-handle height with a pencil and then paint in with a liner brush using F.
With H + D + faux glazing medium (2:1:1), paint in the cast shadows on either side of the door. Soften this effect by rubbing the color off with cheesecloth. That way, the door looks backlit. The shadow is the darkest against the door itself and then washes out as we move away from the door.

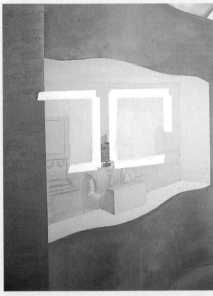

◄ **6** *(Top Left)* Next, paint the concession stand and the soda jerk, whom I affectionately call "Chip."

Block in the face with AA add the facial features and shadows on the left of the face with Z. Base the shirt in FF with EE for shadows in the shirt and DD for the shirt outline. Use GG for reflected light areas around the arm

For the cash register, use F and H. Add Titanium White or a little AA to temper these colors, if need be.

Next, wash in Chip's bowtie with Q.

◄ **7** *(Top Right)* Using a straightedge and pencil, draw the counter, popcorn machine, soda dispenser.

With quick–release tape, mask off the menu board. Then, with a 1–inch (24mm) flat and R, block in the menu board. Dab off as needed with a piece of cheesecloth and add more color back in at the bottom where most of the light comes in.

◄ **8** *(Bottom Left)* Block in the popcorn with a watered–down version of J. Paint the darker popcorn, which is underneath, with M and the lighter popcorn with L. Use O for the lettering on the popcorn machine. Use a wash of Titanium White and water for the glass reflection on the popcorn machine.

Put details on the pop machine with F and D at the bottom and N at the top.

◄ **9** *(Bottom Right)* Next, add more Titanium White to the counter and, using a liner brush and P, put words on the menu board such as hotdog, hamburger, etc. Remember that this is a vintage piece, so only include food items that would have been popular in the 1930's/40's.

Paint the recessed light with S.

◀ **10** Go back with your pencil and re-define the sconce shape (which has been covered over with the green wall color). Block in the sconce with a 1/4-inch (6mm) flat and U. Build up the color in the middle of the sconce in order to simulate the rounded shape. Dab the paint. With a 1-inch (24mm) flat, apply glaze above the sconce and apply V to simulate the light's glow. Dab with cheesecloth to soften the effect.

The shape of this sconce was based on another sconce in the TV room. When doing murals, it goes a long way toward integration of the mural into the room setting if you are able to add actual items from the room into your mural.

◀ **11** Apply more U in the middle of the sconce to further simulate the rounded effect. Paint slots with S—making sure to lighten the color right below as if there were a stream of light escaping.

Next, use W with a 1-inch (24mm) flat and apply a shadow around the bottom perimeter of the sconce. Go back and rub it off for a graduated effect. Apply this same color just inside the sconce perimeter to heighten the rounded effect.

Finally, add texture to the top of the sconce with U.

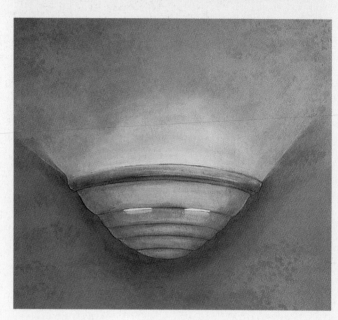

◀ **12** Add more V above the top of the sconce. Dab with cheesecloth to get a muted effect. Use your liner and apply more of the same color immediately above the sconce to enhance the intensity of the light.

▸ **13** Go back to the concession stand and, with a 4-inch (96mm) brush, glaze the entire front of it with color II thinned with a little water and faux glazing medium.

Write the word "snacks" in charcoal and then paint it in with JJ. Apply dots with K, then wipe off charcoal.

▾ **14** *(Bottom Left)* For the floor, go over the grout lines with a pencil and straightedge and rub the lines in a little to simulate grout.

Next, take a no. 8 round and KK mixed with water and faux glazing medium and apply streaks in the floor, using a marbling technique. Drag your brush sideways, twisting the brush as you go. Put dots here and there. Soften this effect by pouncing the marbling with cheesecloth.

As you do the marbling on the floor, keep perspective in mind and be sure to put your streaks closer together at the top, where the floor is farther away and put your streaks farther apart at the bottom of the floor where you are closer in.

▾ **15** *(Bottom Right)* Next, paint the barrier rope. Draw the poles in with pencil using a straightedge. Base the poles in LL and the roping in MM.

Using a no. 3 round, add detailing to metal poles with NN. Next, add a cast shadow with OO.

16 *(Top Left)* For the *Gone with the Wind* poster, basecoat the poster area with Y and then use a book cover or poster as a reference and charcoal in the figures.

17 *(Top Right)* Basecoat the figures, using X for Scarlett's dress, Z for the darker flesh tones and AA for the lighter flesh tones. The hair is HH and the highlight around the figures is GG.

18 *(Bottom Left)* Paint Clark's shirt and the ruffle around Scarlett's décolleté with FF and paint the folds & outlines with EE.
Pencil in the words with charcoal and paint the words in Titanium White.

19 *(Bottom Right)* To create the frame, use quick-release tape and tape off the frame and paint in the frame with DD.

20 *(Top Left)* Add highlights to the frame with a 1/2-inch (12mm) flat and CC using a drybrush technique. Then, using your liner loaded with DD, create a line inside the frame. Finally, add faux glazing mix to DD and put a cast shadow around two sides of the frame.

21 *(Bottom Left)* Using the same palette as with the *Gone with the Wind* poster, approximate the figures of the *Wizard of Oz* poster and paint it. Also, glaze the door with B.

Completed Mural

CLOUDS

project 4

Painting a sky on a ceiling is a popular mural idea because it works so well; it helps to open the space up and provides a kind of joyous feeling to a room. Here, the ceiling was coffered and so the space was broken up. I had to make sure that the cloud rhythms worked despite the interruptions. The client wanted a soft effect so I didn't push the realism too far. It needed a certain amount of believability to work with the wall mural I'd done in the alcove, so I did use shading on the clouds. The birds were added to heighten the sense of illusion and to visually connect the ceiling mural to the wall mural.

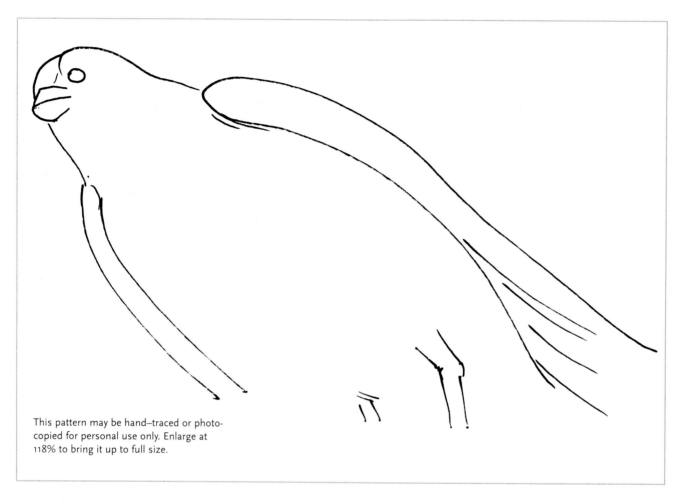

This pattern may be hand–traced or photo-copied for personal use only. Enlarge at 118% to bring it up to full size.

Throughout this project, the colors used will be indicated by the letters shown here.

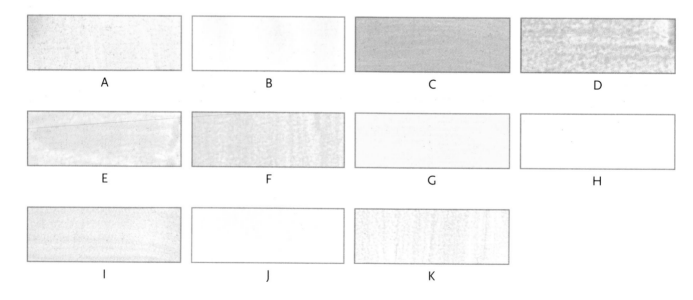

▲ **1** For the ceiling *imprimatura*, use A. With a 2 1/2-inch (60mm) bristle brush, block in the clouds with B. At this stage the painting is sketchy. Let part of the underpainting come through.

▲ **2** When working on such a ceiling job, it is a good idea to have a sample board for color matching rather than trying to do it on the ceiling.

▲ **3** Add C. Spray the clouds with water a little and then use a rag and blot the cloud edges so they're not too sharp.

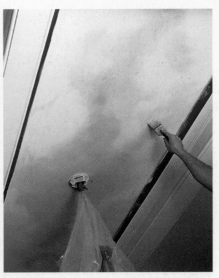

▲ **4** With your 4–inch (96mm) soft bristle brush, add D. Spray with a little water and use a piece of cheesecloth to soften the cloud edges.

▲ **5** Using your 4 1/2–inch (108mm) and 2 1/2–inch (60mm) brushes loaded with Titanium White, use a wet–on–wet technique and paint into the blue of the clouds. Use a sprayer to keep the paint moist during this process.

▲ **6** Using E, add pink to the clouds. Soften the edges with a little clear glazing medium.

▲ **7** Bring C over from the left panel and tie this into the panel with the chandelier.

▲ **8** Paint with B using a slip-slap motion and soften the edges as before.

▲ **9** Using your 2 1/2-inch (60mm) brush, add matte medium to the glaze and add F and darken cloud.

▲ **10** Soften the edges with G.

11 *(Top Right)* With a 1-inch (24mm) and a 2-inch (51mm) brush, use H to accentuate and delineate the cloud puffs.

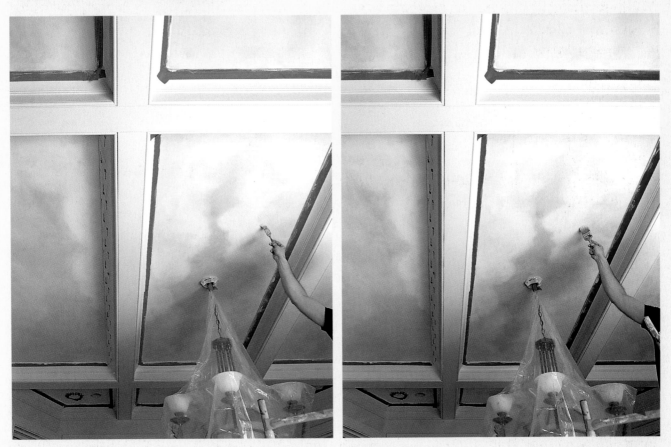

12 With a 1-inch (24mm) brush and color I, add this darker color. This will have the effect of pulling the cloud down.

13 Next, put J around the clouds to soften them.

▲ 14 Go over the grey with K (Pink + White + glaze + matte medium).

If your color gets too warm, just put white right over it to soften the yellow a bit.

▲ 15 First, tape a piece of tracing paper on the ceiling with Quick-Release tape.

▲ 16 Then, draw the goldfinch with charcoal. Here, I used a bird guide as a reference.

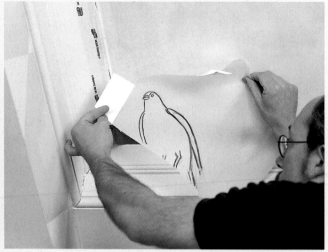

▲ 17 Darken the main lines of the tracing with charcoal so they can be seen easily on the other side. Then, turn over the tracing paper and again trace the main lines of your pattern with charcoal.

▲ **18** Flip the tracing paper over and re-tape in correct direction.

▲ **19** Rub the paper along the outside lines to transfer the charcoal lines of the inside image to the ceiling and then remove the transfer paper.

▲ **20** Here are the completed birds that we added to the cloud mural. For instructions on painting a similar bird, see the Niche project, page 106.

Completed Cloud Mural

Wear a cervical collar to protect your neck.

When using water-based paints, proceed slowly, because they will dry darker.

Avoid making clouds too separate—keep everything fluid.

Keep brushes rolled up in plastic so they don't get dry.

NANTUCKET LIGHTHOUSE

project 5

This client wanted a lighthouse painting to cover a small bathroom window. I suggested a canvas, stretched to fit the space, because I liked the idea of working a traditional scene on canvas, which is easily tacked on a wall for painting and is lightweight for installation (panels are also fine). The composition reflects the verticality of the space; the path leads your eye away from the wall and into the mural. This kind of straightforward scene works well in traditionally decorated homes.

This pattern may be hand-traced or photo-copied for personal use only. Enlarge at 200%, then at 185% to bring to full size.

Throughout this project, the colors used will be indicated by the letters shown here.

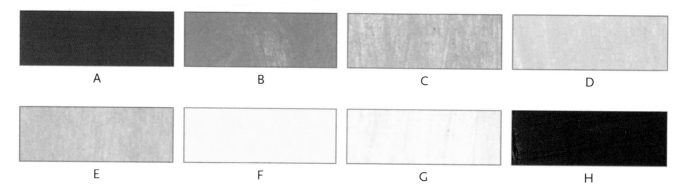

A   B   C   D

E   F   G   H

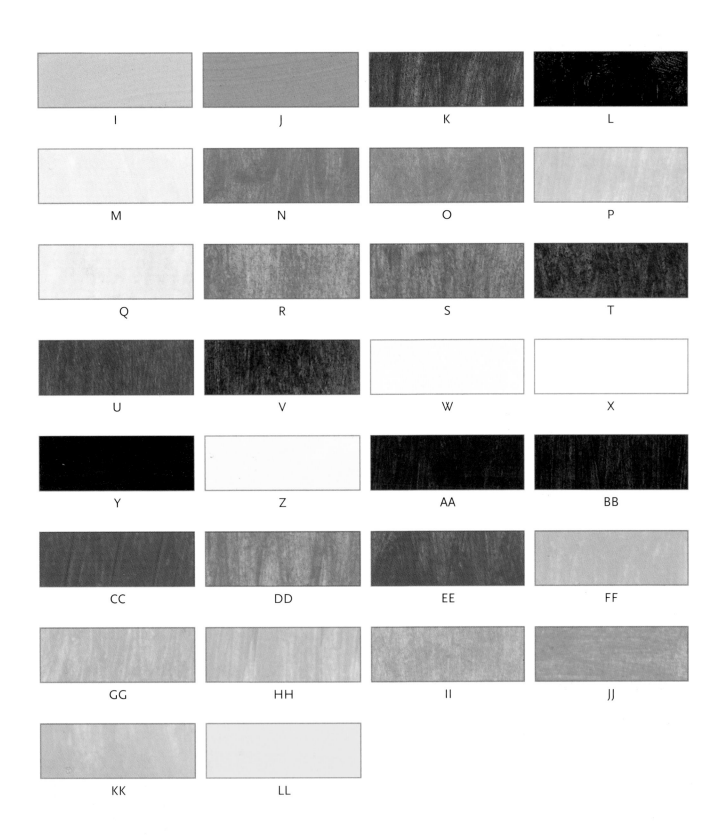

I

J

K

L

M

N

O

P

Q

R

S

T

U

V

W

X

Y

Z

AA

BB

CC

DD

EE

FF

GG

HH

II

JJ

KK

LL

1 *(Left)* Measure the window opening and draw the opening size on a piece of sized canvas. Make sure to keep a border of a couple inches on all sides of the opening in order to be able to pin the piece of canvas up on the wall while painting this movable mural.

Charcoal in the mural and then cartoon the design in with A.

2 *(Right)* Coat the entire canvas with a thinned glazing mixture. This will increase the "open" time while you work.

Paint the sky with B and C and D top to bottom with the horizon color on the bottom.

Tape off the sides of the lighthouse with quick-release tape so the sides stay sharp.

3 Paint the body of the lighthouse with E in the middle, F on the left and G on the right.

4 Paint the top of the lighthouse with H and I and J. Paint the house shingles with K and the windows with L. Use your no. 6 round brush and D to block in the house trim on the roof and M to block in the door and other house trim.

5 *(Left)* Put back the quick-release tape and put in the ocean—starting with N at the bottom and O on the top and streaks of G in the middle.

Put Q on the sand dunes and streak in E to simulate the downward motion.

6 *(Right)* With a 3-inch (72mm) brush, scruff in the grass with R, S, T and V. Base the path with U.

7 Highlight the top of the lighthouse with W and X. Darken under the "crow's nest" walkway with Y. Intensify the highlights on the lighthouse with Q. Lighten the house trim with Z. Use AA to shade around the windows and doors and house trim. Use highlight color Z to create mullions on the windows. Add to the window shadows with BB. Apply CC with a 3/4-inch (18mm) stain brush for the house shingle siding. Use BB to suggest lines of shingles. This needs to have an old, mottled look.

Make sure you know where your light source is when painting your mural.

▲ **8** Make a trellis on the side of the house and the front of the house and on the roof with a no. 6 round and CC. Dab DD on the path in an uneven fashion. Add EE. Paint the picket fence with Z and a no. 6 round.

▲ **9** Paint the leaves on the distant tree with HH and the tree trunk with L.

One of the difficulties in working on landscapes is that you have to create the illusion of depth in your painting. And you must do so convincingly.

In general, foreground elements (those closest to the viewer) are larger, more vibrant in color, and more detailed. Background elements, on the other hand, are smaller, more muted and less distinct.

Keeping this in mind, you have to be careful not to let the beach come too far forward as you add detail. When applying specks to the sand, smudge them with your finger to blend. (This also helps to create a little shadow.)

Then, highlight the foreground grass. This will draw your eye away from the sand.

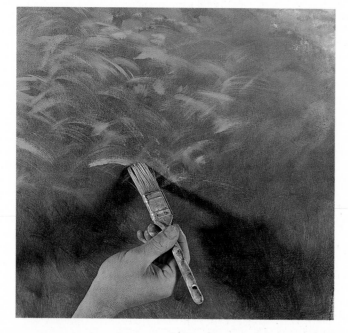

▲ **10** Apply a thin coat of clear glazing medium over the basecoated foreground grass. Then, with FF and GG with clear glazing medium added, apply the rough foreground grass with a 2-inch (51mm) flat brush with a flick of the wrist.

11 *(Left)* Paint climbing rose vines and leaves in GG. Paint the blossoms with II. Lighten the walk with HH.

12 *(Bottom Left)* Use a no. 6 round and GG and apply more grass blades to the foreground. Suggest the brush of the sea roses with KK. Paint the blossoms in with II and JJ. Put in a wash of lighter pink, green, and yellow centers with II, JJ, and KK thinned with water. Put floating blossoms to the right and upper right and go back and add wispy branches and leaves on those flowers like we did with the other ones.

Use LL and paint yellow center in the sea roses. Use Q and J to detail the beach.

Finished canvas, mounted in window.

CHLOE'S ROOM

project 6

I designed this mural to fit this specific type of ceiling. The simplicity of the stripes is meant to prevent the ceiling from appearing to bear down on the viewer. I invented the bamboo armature to introduce both the golden color and a fun shape for a little girl's bedroom like this one. The golden fringe is also for fun and to accent the rather simple stripes. The pink bows and purple flowers (Chloe's favorite colors) were put in to soften the mural, add visual interest, and aid in the illusion of a large tent over the room.

Throughout this project, the colors used will be indicated by the letters shown here.

This pattern may be hand–traced or photocopied for personal use only. Enlarge at 200%, then at 111% to bring to full size.

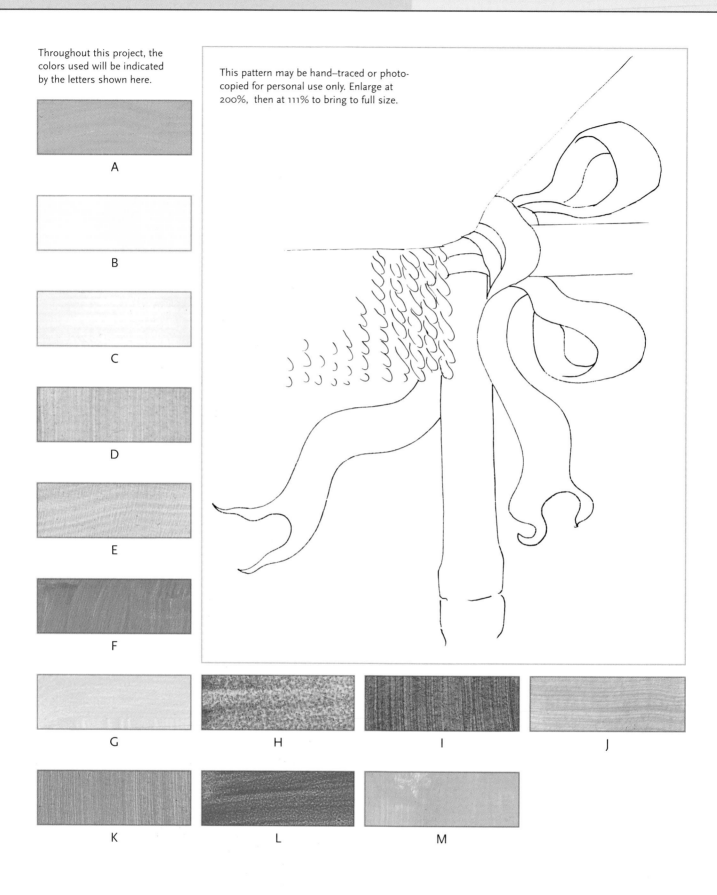

A

B

C

D

E

F

G

H

I

J

K

L

M

This pattern may be hand–traced or photo-copied for personal use only. Enlarge at 192% to bring it up to full size.

▲ **1** Paint the background color using a 4-inch (96mm) brush and C. Use a level and tape off the bottom edge of what will replicate a tent structure and pencil off vertical lines with the level and a red pencil.

▲ **2** Using a 3-inch (72mm) brush and A mixed with clear glazing medium, apply alternating stripes, daubing with cheesecloth to soften the effect a bit.

▲ **3** Paint the second stripe with B. Wipe excess color off with a wet cloth as desired.

▲ **4** Using your no. 8 round loaded with D, visualize rope and paint angled oval dots—one right on top of the other—to simulate this. Try not to be too uniform with them. Also, make sure that the individual strands of fringe sway back and forth and aren't static and totally straight. Use this same color to stipple on a line between the bottom of the stripes and the fringe.

Your lines don't have to be perfectly straight. As a matter of fact, it adds character to have somewhat imperfect lines. However, if you do want to be more exact, feel free to use masking tape.

After taking the tape off, you might have to add some bottom strokes to the fringe so that it's not too perfectly straight. Or, you might just want to use a penciled-in line instead of the tape.

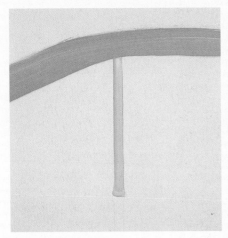

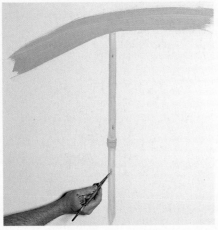

▲ **5** In order to create the bamboo pole, outline the pole shape with a red pencil and use your 1/2-inch (12mm) flat brush loaded with D + clear glazing medium + water (2:1:1) to base it in.

▲ **6** Next, apply E + clear glazing medium (1:1) to bamboo stick and then take a piece of slightly damp cheesecloth and take some paint off in the middle of the pole in order to create a highlight, which gives the illusion of a rounded shape. Add the bamboo knots.

▲ **7** Lightly sketch in the ribbons and ties with charcoal. Use a 1/2–inch (12mm) flat brush and F to paint in the bows. Highlight with G using a no. 4 flat. Further highlight by adding Titanium White.

▲ **9** Use your no. 4 flat stain brush to paint leaves with L. Use M for the highlights.

▲ **8** Use no. 6 round stain brush and H to draw in the vine. With your no. 5 round and no. 1 flat stain brush, lay in the fuchsia flowers with I and use J as a highlight. Use K for the orange petals.

SQUIRREL

project 7

Single animals like our furry friend here are great subjects to place in unusual spaces in rooms to liven things up and add a bit of fun, without the size or expense of larger murals. Putting a squirrel (or a bird or a monkey) over a door is very popular with clients and the fact that it may not be noticed by people at first is part of its charm.

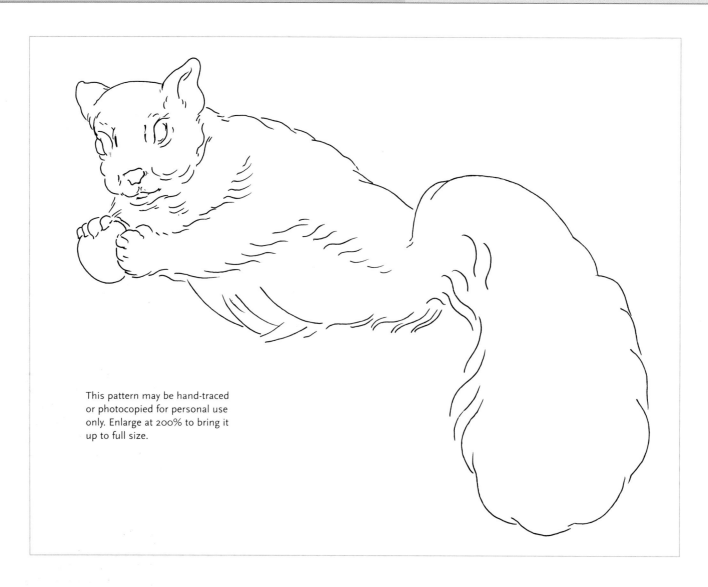

This pattern may be hand-traced or photocopied for personal use only. Enlarge at 200% to bring it up to full size.

Throughout this project, the colors used will be indicated by the letters shown here.

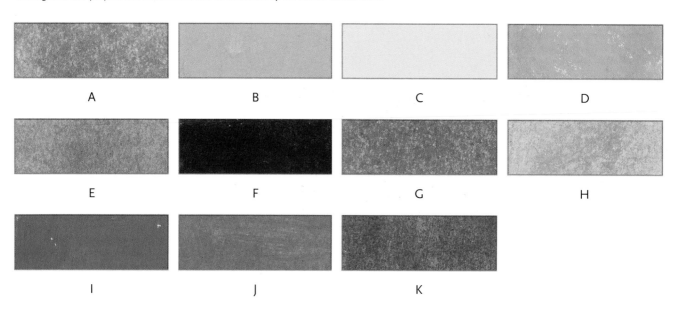

▲ **1** *(Top Left)* Either use the pattern and transfer the design to the wall or freehand your squirrel with charcoal. Then, using your no. 6 round brush and A, cartoon the design onto the wall.

▲ **2** *(Top Right)* Next, with a no. 10 flat stain brush loaded with a wash of E + water, wash in this color over the entire squirrel.

◀ **3** With your no. 12 shader, block in the shadow areas with I.

▲ **4** (*Above Left*) Then create texture in the fur with your no. 4 round stain brush and B.

▲ **5** (*Above Right*) Now, load your no. 5 round brush, with F & J, add detail and darken the eyes, hands and ears and anywhere else you feel you need to add darkened accents.

◄ **6** Next, still using your no. 5 round brush, use C to put in highlights. For the fur technique, make sure the paint is thinned with water. Move your entire arm and pull in directional strokes for the fur.

When you texture, the paint will lighten a little as it dries. Don't worry. You can re-apply this value and build up the color.

▲ **7** *(Top Left)* Base the berry with your no. 6 round brush loaded with K. Put a wash of G over the dark areas with your no. 12 shader. Then, highlight the berry with your no. 6 round loaded with D.

▲ **8** *(Top Right)* Finally, load your no. 12 shader with H thinned with water. Put this wash on the squirrel to warm up the color. Add more highlights if desired with C.

Finished Squirrel

NICHE

project 8

Painted architectural illusions are a great way to "open-up" walls and create visual interest. They also add an element of fun. I used source material to find a niche that I liked (combining elements from two images) and used a compass and a bendable, curved plastic drawing tool for the top. I drew one half of the niche and then used the tracing paper transfer method to copy that onto the other half to make sure that it was symmetrical. You don't have to be an architect to do this: I never fuss too much over being absolutely exact. Proper shading can hide many flaws! This niche is painted monochromatically to mimic stone and the bird was added at the client's request: I purposely chose a small bird so that I could add a nest.

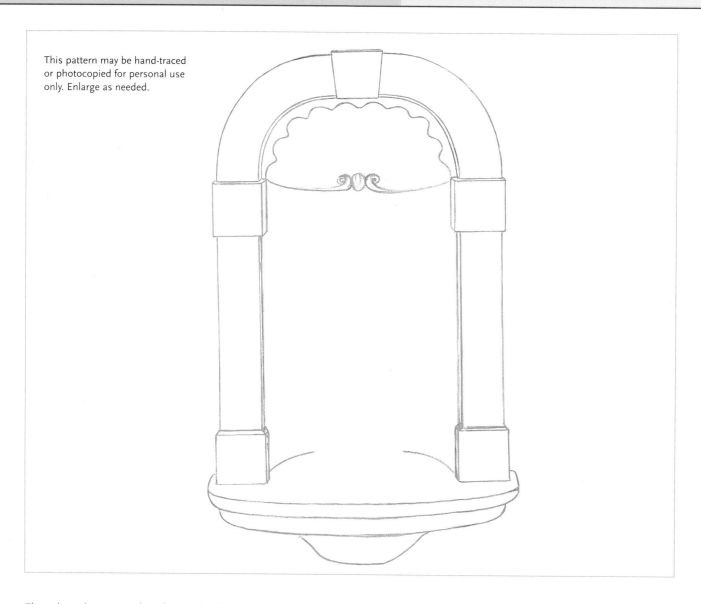

This pattern may be hand-traced
or photocopied for personal use
only. Enlarge as needed.

Throughout this project, the colors used will be indicated by the letters shown here.

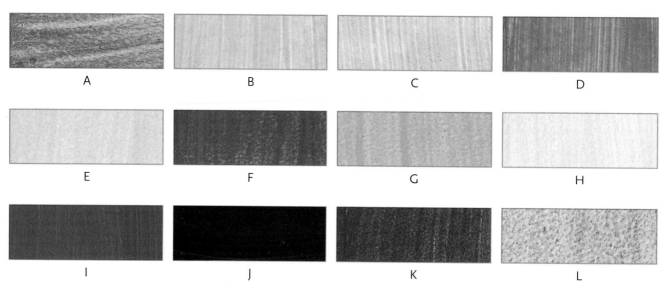

◀ **1** *(Top Left)* Transfer the niche pattern onto your surface (here I am using a piece of canvas) using charcoal.

Use A thinned (but not runny) to paint over the charcoal lines.

With your 2–inch (51mm) brush, wipe the surface with a mix of glaze + water (4:1) to make the surface smoother. Next, apply glaze + a wash of B and C to basecoat the niche. Then, wipe off some paint in order to achieve a mottled appearance.

◀ **2** *(Top Right)* With a combination of small flat brushes and medium round brushes loaded with D, shade the shell motif.

◀ **3** Add highlighting with E.

▲ **5** Transfer the pattern of the yellow–rumped warbler and nest in charcoal. Brush-sketch the bird in with a no. 3 round loaded with F.

▲ **6** Base in the bird with G, H, I and J. Base in the nest with K. Put a shadow under the bird with K.

▲ **7** Add the eggs with I and G, then highlight the nest with B and D.

▲ **8** Next, use your 1 1/2–inch (36mm) flat brush loaded with L and glaze the niche. For this step, you should choose spots on the niche which you can scruff up, such as the edges and the back of the niche. This adds a three–dimensional effect. Now add a shadow under the niche with L.

Photo: Greg Matulionis

EGRETS

project 9

This mural involves two problems at once: an unusual open-ended wall space to work on and a need to appear both Western and oriental in style. I dealt with the former by letting the edges fade off in an irregular fashion. Stylistically, the painting has spatial effects and the modeling of form common to Western Art but it also suggests the verticality and some of the stylized effects (angular forms, emphasis on outlines, darkly-shaded edges) of Eastern Art.

Throughout this project, the colors used will be indicated by the letters shown here.

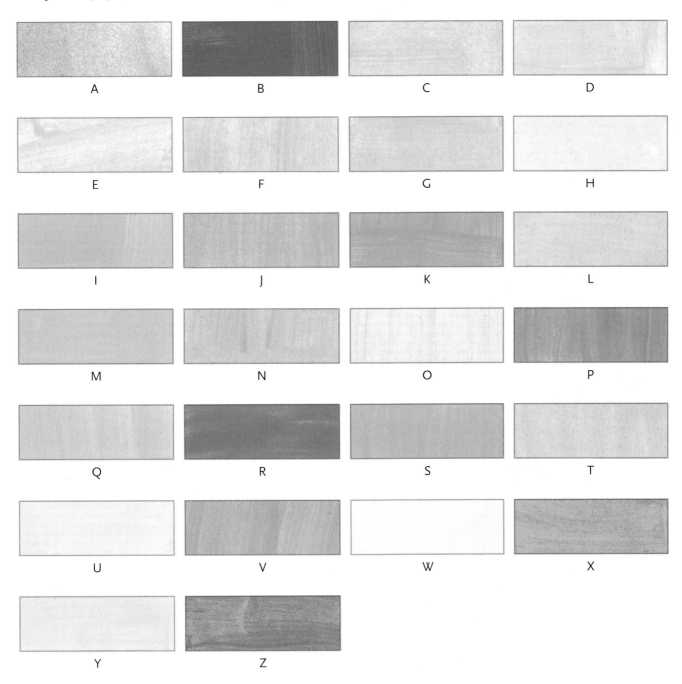

▲ **1** Charcoal in the design and then cartoon it in with B. Add water to that same color and use it to wash in the tree trunks and nest. Wash the water in with thinned C and D.

▲ **2** Use B and E to base in the trees at the top. Put F on the tree groups to the left and right of the original grouping. Use G for the lower tree groupings near the cliffs. Use I for the lowest tree groupings. With your 1–inch (24mm) brush, stipple the color on and smoosh it with a rag for texture and to fade out.

Use J in the lower left and right corners and use K and L for the bushes in the lowest area of foliage.

▲ **3** Use M for the sandy shore. Paint the cliffs with N and paint the water in with O.

The mural is starting to get an oriental feel. In order to create this feeling, your strokes should be angular along the horizontal line and have a grid-type look. The limbs are angular.

▲ **4** *(Above Left)* Use the blue and green hues (C & H) mixed with the matte medium for the water reflections.

With your 1/2-inch (12mm) flat loaded with P, put in more Japanese-like foliage on the lower left of the mural.

Add water to M and wash in the pagoda. Then, darken it with B. Darken the boat and upper branch of the tree on the left with B.

▲ **5** *(Above Right)* Next, block in the nest with 1-inch (24mm) and 2-inch (51mm) brushes and Q and R. You may want to use the no. 10 flat on top of the nest.

◄ **6** Now, use B and go over the branches and paint twigs on the nest.

▲ **7** *(Top Left)* Highlight the twigs in the nest with S, T, and U. Next, paint the egrets (adults & babies) with V and W.

▲ **8** *(Top Right)* Paint in the egret beaks with X and Y.

◄ **9** *(Left)* Using a no. 8 round and B, draw vertical lines for the willow branches on which the leaves will be placed. With your 3/8-inch (10mm) angle brush, loaded with Z, paint the willow leaves.

Completed egret mural

Photo: Greg Matulionis

FRENCH TRELLIS

project 10

The emphasis here was on softness. The client and I both agreed that the trellis should enhance the dining room without calling too much attention to itself. I did this by carefully mixing a gray for the trellis lath—like the gray of the trellises found at Versailles—which blended perfectly with the surroundings. Then I kept the values light in order to emphasize subtlety. I placed the vines and flowers in an unfussy arrangement intended to give rhythm to the whole while contrasting with the geometry of the trellis. I also designed the crown of the trellis to provide needed curves to echo the door moldings and to draw your eye away from the corner.

This pattern may be hand-traced or photo-copied for personal use only. Enlarge at 200%, then at 163% to bring to full size.

Throughout this project, the colors used will be indicated by the letters shown here.

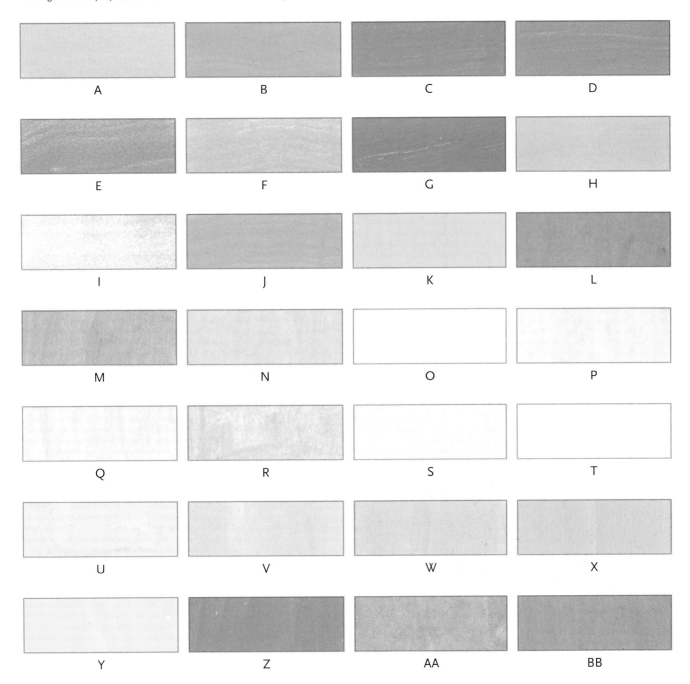

A B C D

E F G H

I J K L

M N O P

Q R S T

U V W X

Y Z AA BB

1 *(Top Left)* Tape off the straight lines of the trellis with quick-release tape and transfer the pattern for the rounded, top part of the trellis with charcoal.

2 *(Top Right)* Load your 3/4-inch (19mm) flat brush with a mix of A thinned with water (5:1) and paint in the trellis lath.

3 With your no. 5 round loaded with B, shade the underside of the trellis lath as if there were shadows there. To do this, you will have to decide where your light source is and shade appropriately. You may want to use a straight edge for this step.

4 Lay in the camellia leaves with a 3/4-inch (19mm) flat brush loaded with C. Take your brush and swish a stroke on the left and then swish one on the right in order to create your leaf.

▲ **5** Next, lay in the passionflower leaves with D and your 3/4-inch (19mm) flat brush.

▲ **6** For the camellia, use your 1/2-inch (12mm) wash brush and base the flower with K. Now, with your no. 1 round stain brush, draw the petal outlines with L.

With your no. 2 round stain brush, add shadows to petals with M. Add highlights with your no. 1 round stain brush and N. Finally, add white highlights with O using the wet-on-wet method with your no. 1 round stain brush. Re-draw the red outlines if needed.

▲ **7** To create the passion-flower, use your no. 4 round stain brush and base in half the flower petals with U and half with W. Base in the center of the flower with Y. With a no. 6 round brush, shade in the petals. For U, use V; for W use X. Shade the centers with a no. 1 round stain brush and BB. Using your 10/0 round brush, paint the pistil and stamen details with Z. Finally, with your no. 1 round stain brush, accentuate the petal outlines and shadows with X and Z.

9 *(Top Left)* To create the vines for the camellia flowers, use E and start with a no. 6 round at the bottom of the trellis. Try to make it look like the vines start behind the trellis and come forward. You will need to switch to a no. 3 round brush about halfway up the trellis, as the vine would naturally become smaller.

Next, add Titanium White to E and highlight the vines where the sun would naturally hit them.

10 *(Top Right)* Now, add the vines for the passionflowers with the no. 6 round and F. Do this in the same way you did for the camellias, but be sure to make the growth habit of this vine a little different from the first one, since this is a different plant.

11 For the clematis leaves, use your no. 3 round loaded with G. Create leaves with serrated edges.

12 For the clematis flower, block in the flower with your no. 6 round and P. Add contrasting color Q. Shade with R. Using your no. 2 round stain brush, highlight with S. Add white highlights into the previous color with T using the wet-on-wet method.

At this point, the owner decided she wanted more flowers and thought that blue would be a nice complement to the other colors in the room, so we chose a clematis flower, the C. Alpina "Frances Rivis" which is different from most better known clematis flowers. It looks more like a snowdrop or an Alpine wildflower.

▲ **13** Now, add the clematis vine with a no. 6 round loaded with H. Again, you may want to switch to a smaller brush about halfway up the trellis as the vines would naturally get smaller. This is the third vine on the trellis. Make sure it turns and twists a bit differently from the other two so that it's obvious there are three distinct vines.

▲ **14** Load your no. 6 round with I and create more shadows on the trellis. This gives definition and depth to the structure and makes it more convincing.

◀ **15** Finally, load your 1/4-inch (6mm) flat glaze brush and highlight the leaves with J.

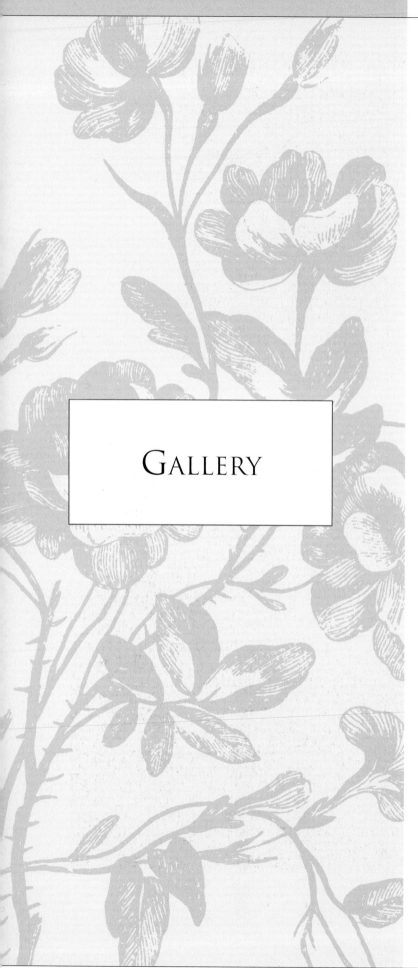

GALLERY

The photographic gallery that follows shows a variety of murals that I've done under varying circumstances. It's certainly a pleasure to be able to present them here to the readers of this book. I have my favorites, of course, but basically it is always a satisfying experience to see a finished mural photographed in a completely decorated setting. More often than not, when I leave the room where I've just finished painting a mural, things are in disarray: tables and chairs have been moved about; pictures aren't hung; the final décor is yet to be realized. This is especially true in new construction or remodeling situations. Although the artist is almost always one of the last people brought in on such a job, much still remains to be done after the paint has dried.

Another of the pleasures of seeing a picture gallery like the one that follows is being able to see the consistencies of style throughout the work, despite the variety of subject matter. I especially enjoy noticing those stylistic touches that are completely intuitive.

Naturally, like any artist, I inevitably come across portions of past murals that I would like to tweak a bit. I've read about more than one artist bringing paints into people's houses to redo sections of their paintings that had been hanging for years!

This American landscape is in the dining room of the residence of Mr. & Mrs. Tim Brown.

This landscape mural is in the home of Mr. & Mrs. Todd Stegman.

The Pompeii Room is in the home of Mr. & Mrs. John Barbara

This dining room mural is an example of an early American landscape.

This Indonesian scene is in Teak restaurant, Cincinnati, Ohio.

This fantasy Medieval scene is in the Kenton County public library, Covington, Kentucky.

This cityscape is in the boardroom of the CSX Railroad, Midwest Division—headquartered in Cincinnati, Ohio.

This safari-themed mural is in a model home in Erlanger, Kentucky.

RENDERINGS

enderings of murals have a variety of purposes. Most importantly, they allow a client the opportunity to get a clearer sense of what the mural is to look like. Many people have a difficult time envisioning a wall painting from the verbal description alone. I often ask clients to provide visual aids to help begin the creative process. They usually find it easy to point out things that appeal to them and they may even say something like: "This is sort of what I have in mind...but maybe it could be brighter...."

After an initial meeting, a client is left with a business card and/or a brochure. This is not much help for visualizing a mural. Providing them with a rendering is the next logical step. It gives them something tangible to live with for a while in order to give better feedback when you next get together.

Most of my renderings are basically drawings done in scale to the final wall painting. I do not automatically provide color renderings, unless asked to do so. After the initial pencil sketch or monochromatic drawing, the client may request something in color and/or in greater detail.

I always do my renderings on high quality water-color drawing paper, usually in gouache, and I sign and label them with the appropriate job title, such as "Rendering for Dining Room Mural—Smith Residence." I present them as works of art—not just something torn out of a sketchbook.

VENETIAN MURAL

In this rendering, I started with the architectural elements and used an overlay to add different Venetian vistas from which the client chose his preferred version.

ORIENTAL LANDSCAPE

This client provided several pieces of framed artwork from which certain images were chosen and incorporated into the mural.

(Above) This rendering is very close to the completed mural.

(Right) The completed version of this ceiling is much more impressionistic.

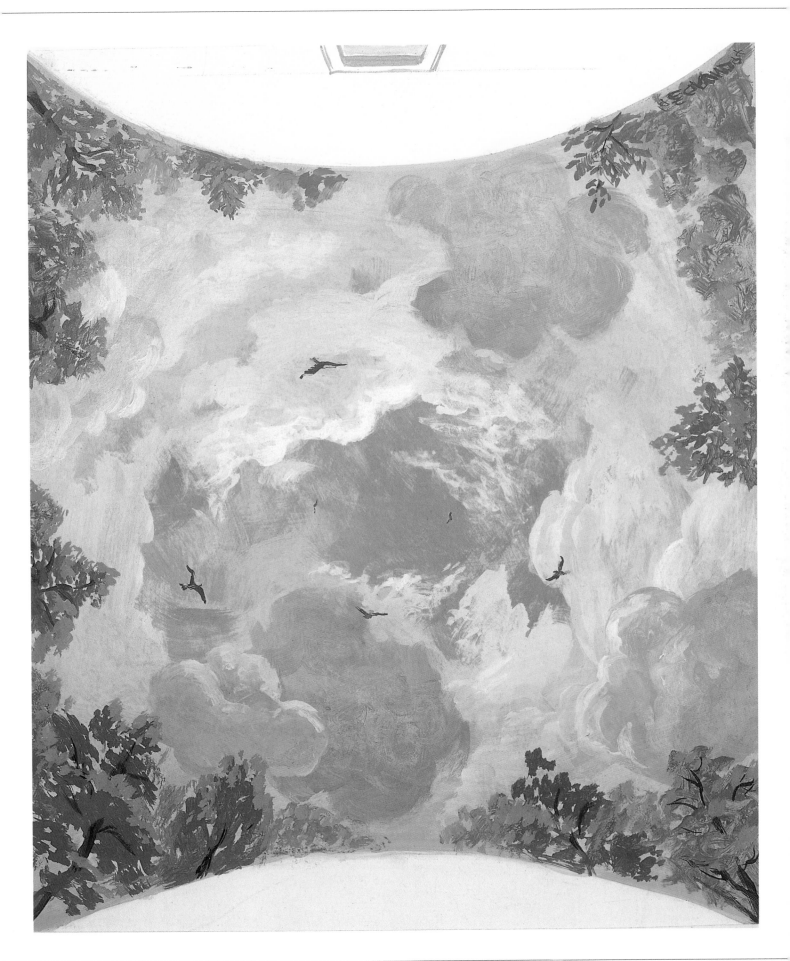

MANOR HOUSE

This rendering was created for a twelve by sixty-foot movable wall in a banquet center. The sheer scale of this mural greatly influenced my design.

THE UNIVERSITY CLUB

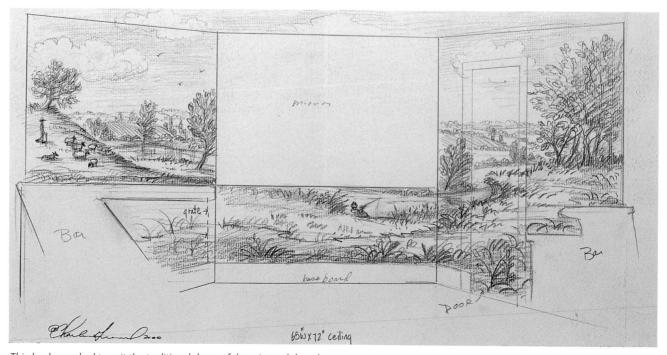

This landscape had to suit the traditional decor of the private club and had to work in an unusual enclosed space.

FRENCH LANDSCAPE

These clients were very particular about the authenticity of this landscape. The design had to take into account door openings, turns in the wall and a fireplace. (See completed mural, page 127—top.)

This client wanted a Chagall-like feeling to the mural in her baby's room. The color swatches are an attempt to match colors of fabric already in the room.

FRENCH LANDSCAPE

This is the kind of rendering I often give to a client to represent a rough idea. If needed, I will subsequently do a more detailed and/or full-colored version for the client. (See rendering, page 139 and completed mural, page 127.)

GENERAL SUPPLIES

ASW Art Supply Warehouse
5325 Departure Dr.
Raleigh, NC 27616-1835
1-800-995-6778
www.aswexpress.com

Daniel Smith
P.O. Box 84268
Seattle, Washington 98124-5568
1-800-426-6740
www.danielsmith.com

Dick Blick Art Materials
P.O. Box 1267
Galesburg, Illinois 61402-1267
1-800-828-4548
www.dickblick.com

Flax art & design
240 Valley Drive
Brisbane, California 94005-1206
1-800-343-3529
askus@flaxart.com

Jerry's Artarama
Order Department
P.O. Box 58638J
Raleigh, NC 27658-8638
1-800-827-8478
www.jerryscatalog.com

New York Central Art Supply
62 Third Avenue
New York, New York 10003
1-800-950-6111
sales@nycentral.com

Pearl Paint
308 Canal Street
New York, New York 10013
1-800-221-6845
www.pearlpaint.com

Utrecht
332 South Michigan Avenue
Chicago, Illinois 60604
1-312-922-7565
utrechtart.com

BRUSHES

Elder & Jenks
148 East 5th Street
Bayonne, New Jersey 07002
1-800-631-3440

Loew-Cornell
563 Chestnut Avenue
Teaneck, New Jersey 07666-2490
Loew-cornell@loew-cornell.com

PAINT

Benjamin Moore & Co.
51 Chestnut Ridge Road
Montvale, New Jersey 07645
1-800-344-0400
benjaminmoore@att.net.

Golden Artist Colors
188 Bell Road
New Berlin, New York 13411-9527
Technical assistance: 1-800-959-6543
orderinfo@goldenpaints.com

East Providence Public Library
East Providence Public Library
Weaver Memorial Library

JUL   2003

No Longer Property of
East Providence Public Library

PAINTING MURALS STEP BY STEP

East Providence Public Library
Weaver Memorial Library